"*A Psychoanalytic Study of Political Leadership in the United States and Russia: Searching for Truth* presents an important approach to political discourse. Edited by psychologist and psychoanalyst Karyne E. Messina, the book's essays explore the need to seek truth and reasons for behavior of political actors.

Messina provides an essential contextual setting in American and Russian history that led to the current situation of a new Cold War and a hot war in Ukraine. She also stresses the need to distinguish what we know and do not know about Vladimir Putin.

Dr. Harry Gill looks at the war from the perspective of Eastern Europeans, who have seen many internecine conflicts and shifting borders. He warns of the danger of oversimplifying the relationships by fitting them into solely Western constructs of how the world works.

The historian Peter W. Petschauer delves into Putin's biography for clues into his behavior. Childhood traumas and a longing for a stable regime, evinced in his reading, influenced Putin's development.

Psychoanalyst Vamik Volkan and psychologist Jana Javakhishvili examine leader-follower relationships and Putin's leadership style. Does he follow in the footsteps of such dictators as Stalin and Milosevic?

Quantitative research by psychologist Robert Gordon compares the mental functioning of Putin, Trump, and Zelensky, presenting a matrix to judge authoritarian behavior and intellectual stability.

Novelist Austin Ratner looks at Putin through the lens of Russian literature, showing that *The Brothers Karamazov* by Dostoevsky is not a paean to Russian imperialism and should not be seen as a paradigm for modern politics.

An important aspect of this study is that the authors are women and men who come from backgrounds that give them a different point of view on both America and Russia, an experience of war and confrontation that many writers about Putin lack. Their combined insights, coming from various angles, build a picture that teaches us that we must examine not only the psychology of world leaders but our own as well, to understand the reasons for our willingness to accept easy and incendiary answers instead of doing independent research and thinking. Reason and respect may yet save the world."

Antonina W. Bouis *is an award-winning translator of Russian literature. She was the founding director of the Soros Foundations during the perestroika in the Soviet Union. She is on the board of the Andrei Sakharov Foundation and Track Two: An Institute for Citizen Diplomacy at Esalen. Member of the Council on Foreign Relations and PEN*

"*A Psychoanalytic Study of Political Leadership in the United States and Russia: Searching for Truth*, edited by Dr Karyne Messina, who also contributes several chapters, is an important study. The book begins with a psychoanalytically informed exploration of why truth is essential in a democracy. Messina makes the case that we can use factual and even historical evidence as well as external expressions of leadership such as documents and treaties to understand world leaders and their underlying psychology. This forms the backdrop for understanding what is going on in present-day Russia under the leadership of Vladimir Putin, as well as his relationship with the United States and the war he instigated in Ukraine. One of the strengths of the book is that it uses multiple methods of inquiry ranging from historical to quantitative analyses, qualitative case history, and literary analysis."

Kevin Volkan, *EdD, PhD, MPH, Professor of Psychology at California State University Channel Islands; Adjunct Professor of Clinical Psychology, California Lutheran University; Medical Education Faculty, Community Memorial Health Systems*

"Psychologist-Psychoanalyst Karyne Messina takes us on a personal odyssey from youthful illusionment to mature disillusionment with American political leadership. Becoming aware, at least by the time she studied at university, that her generally honest father was capable of 'unnecessary' narcissistic lies, she eventually realized how widespread such lying was among major American political 'parent figures.' She usefully informs or reminds readers of the lies President Truman told 'justifying' the US atomic bombing of Japan, claiming we were attacking military bases, as opposed to terrorizing civilian populations to undermine morale, much like Putin does in Ukraine. She also reminds us of the lies President Johnson and Defense Secretary McNamara told to justify our killing of over 5 million people in Viet Nam; Reagan's lies denying sending illegal weapons to Iran; lies about the My Lai rape and massacre; lies about torture at Abu Ghraib; President Biden's lies; and on it goes. Dr. Messina ends with a passionate plea for truth-telling, very much including facing up to lies and atrocities we have already perpetrated. Her opening chapter is almost a page-turner, almost a murder mystery. In fact, it is a murder mystery. In it, disturbingly, we meet the mass murdering group, and we are part of it.

Messina's second chapter provides a balanced overview of the personal, historical, and sociopolitical motives for Putin's serial invasions of Ukraine. She underscores NATO's betrayal of Russia via not living up to promises to not expand NATO 'one inch' beyond Germany into countries formerly controlled by the Soviet Union.

Historian Peter Petschauer situates Putin in a long-term temporal context. He provides interesting hints of possible effects of the Russian President's possible identifications with Russian historical figures, some of whom were extremely brutal within and outside their families. Petschauer notes that Putin abused his first wife.

Psychoanalyst Vamik Volkan and psychologist Jana Javakhishvili contribute a chapter on leader–follower relationships. They usefully remind us that Soviet officials in 1932–1933 confiscated the entire grain supply from eastern and central Ukrainian villages and closed the roads to restrict movement. In this Holodomor (Ukrainian term meaning 'to kill by starvation'), approximately four and a half million people died. (Putin follows in this 'strongman, savior' tradition, favoring genocide to acquire resources.) Volkan and Javakhishvili wonder if Putin aspires to become more well-known and 'important' than Stalin, his House of Horrors predecessor. They place Putin in the context of other totalitarians, like Milosevic, who foster a sense of victimization, followed by a sense of entitlement for revenge, leading to genocidal acts.

Stating that malignant mental illness of autocratic leaders causes the worst possible, avoidable suffering, psychologist Robert Gordon argues that it is the duty of experts to educate and warn of such dangers. Approximately 190,000,000 died due to the leadership of Hitler, Stalin, and Mao, and our tendency to follow these idealized, charismatic, alpha males. Gordon and his colleagues' rating scale research points to extreme liabilities in Putin and Trump (versus mental health assets in Zelenskyy).

In a very creative essay, novelist and physician Austin Ratner looks at Putin through the lens of Russian literature, lamenting that if only Putin could have learned more about psychological development from these brilliant authors, we would not be suffering his horrific invasion of Ukraine.

Harry Gill, a physician and neuroscientist of East European origin, stresses the disastrous consequences of not understanding opponents' psychological, historical, cultural, religious, and economic perspectives. Our preference for simplistic narratives has cost millions of lives and trillions of dollars. We are slow to learn from history and experience. Gill pleads with us to give up our fondness for simply demonizing our opponents. We must replace that stance with communication, validation, compromise, empathy – a willingness to walk a mile in their shoes – ingredients that have proved so important in all therapeutic relationships.

Messina bookends this volume with a plea for evidence-based truth-telling to establish trust. She usefully reminds readers of Bion's concept of the alpha function needed to transform others' anxiety and our own into something workable. A Truth and Reconciliation process may be required as a container for promoting this necessary transmogrification and evolution.

Dr. Karyne Messina has brought together a welcome diversity of voices, creating a powerful conceptual choir. This volume contains something for every reader interested in the never-ending geopolitical crises we create and encounter as we blunder blindly from one disaster to the next. This chorale's diversity will challenge those of us whose position may be insufficiently comprehensive, and likely will be constructively stimulating, expanding understanding in necessary ways. In the diverse views of this multidisciplinary group, there are similarities and differences – a state of affairs calling for what I have elsewhere termed a *comparative-integrative* perspective. Messina's collective offers us a wealth of facts, ideas, perspectives, and crucial concepts needed to help us emerge from our otherwise endless repetition compulsion in which we continue destroying millions of lives, and squandering trillions of dollars' worth of valuable resources. The gauntlet has been thrown down in front of us. Will we rise to the occasion, or opt to continue in our catastrophic ways?"

Brent Willock, *Ph.D. has had a distinguished career as a psychologist and psychoanalyst. He is the Chief Psychologist at the Hincks Treatment Center in Toronto and has been an adjunct faculty member at York University as well as an associate faculty member in the School of Graduate Studies at the University of Toronto*

A Psychoanalytic Study of Political Leadership in the United States and Russia

A Psychoanalytic Study of Political Leadership in the United States and Russia: Searching for Truth provides psychoanalytic insight into the motives of this complex and contradictory figure.

The contributors, from different professional and academic backgrounds, use a range of methods including quantitative research and literary analysis to shed light on Putin's background, outlook and current actions. Reflecting a range of perspectives on how Putin's background may have informed his beliefs and his actions, particularly with respect to the invasion of Ukraine, the book brings together diverse viewpoints.

A Psychoanalytic Study of Political Leadership in the United States and Russia will be of great interest to psychoanalysts and to readers seeking to understand the complex dynamics of populist leadership.

Karyne E. Messina, Ed.D., is a licensed psychologist and psychoanalyst, and is on the medical staff of Suburban Hospital in Bethesda, Maryland. She is a Training and Supervision Analyst at the Washington Baltimore Center for Psychoanalysis. Her books include *Misogyny, Projective Identification and Mentalization: Psychoanalytic, Social and Institutional Manifestations* and *Resurgence of Global Populism: A Psychoanalytic Study of Blame-Shifting and the Corruption of Democracy*.

A Psychoanalytic Study of Political Leadership in the United States and Russia

Searching for Truth

Edited by Karyne E. Messina

LONDON AND NEW YORK

Designed cover image: © Getty

First published 2024
by Routledge
4 Park Square, Milton Park, Abingdon, Oxon OX14 4RN

and by Routledge
605 Third Avenue, New York, NY 10158

Routledge is an imprint of the Taylor & Francis Group, an informa business

© 2024 selection and editorial matter, Karyne E. Messina individual chapters, the contributors

The right of Karyne E. Messina to be identified as the author of the editorial material, and of the authors for their individual chapters, has been asserted in accordance with sections 77 and 78 of the Copyright, Designs and Patents Act 1988.

All rights reserved. No part of this book may be reprinted or reproduced or utilised in any form or by any electronic, mechanical, or other means, now known or hereafter invented, including photocopying and recording, or in any information storage or retrieval system, without permission in writing from the publishers.

Trademark notice: Product or corporate names may be trademarks or registered trademarks, and are used only for identification and explanation without intent to infringe.

British Library Cataloguing-in-Publication Data
A catalogue record for this book is available from the British Library

Library of Congress Cataloguing-in-Publication Data
Names: Messina, Karyne E., author.
Title: A psychoanalytic study of political leadership in the United States and Russia : searching for truth / [edited by] Karyne E. Messina.
Description: Abingdon, Oxon ; New York, NY : Routledge, 2024. | Includes bibliographical references and index. |
Identifiers: LCCN 2024005364 (print) | LCCN 2024005365 (ebook) | ISBN 9781032637792 (hardback) | ISBN 9781032637747 (paperback) | ISBN 9781032637822 (ebook)
Subjects: LCSH: Political leadership--Psychological aspects. | Political leadership--Russia (Federation) | Political leadership--United States. | Putin, Vladimir Vladimirovich, 1952---Psychology.
Classification: LCC JC330.3 .P78 2024 (print) | LCC JC330.3 (ebook) | DDC 324.2447/012--dc23/eng/20240220
LC record available at https://lccn.loc.gov/2024005364
LC ebook record available at https://lccn.loc.gov/2024005365

ISBN: 978-1-032-63779-2 (hbk)
ISBN: 978-1-032-63774-7 (pbk)
ISBN: 978-1-032-63782-2 (ebk)

DOI: 10.4324/9781032637822

Typeset in Times New Roman
by MPS Limited, Dehradun

Contents

Acknowledgments   xi
Preface   xii

Introduction   1

PART 1
Looking Within   5

1 Why the Truth is Essential in a Democracy: Pivoting Toward Evidence   7
KARYNE E. MESSINA

2 Observations, Knowledge, and Speculation: What We *Know* and *Don't Know* About Vladimir Putin   29
KARYNE E. MESSINA

PART 2
Understanding Vladimir Putin from an Eastern European Perspective   59

3 Interpreting Vladimir Putin from Afar Leads to Over-Simplification of Very Complex Relationships   61
HARRY GILL

PART 3
Investigating Vladimir Putin's Personality: How Trauma Affected His Development   73

4 Zeitenwende: Vladimir Putin's Effort to Reestablish
   the Russian/Post-Soviet Empire   75
   PETER W. PETSCHAUER

5 Invasion of Ukraine: Observations on
   Leader–Follower Relationships   83
   VAMIK VOLKAN AND JANA D. JAVAKHISHVILI

PART 4
Quantitative Research Conducted by a Preeminent Researcher   101

6 Measuring the Mental Functioning of Putin,
   Trump, and Zelensky   103
   ROBERT M. GORDON

PART 5
A Scholar Looks at Vladimir Putin through the Lens of Russian Literature   121

7 Dear Vladimir Putin: If You've Read Dostoyevsky,
   You've Tragically Misunderstood Him—Austin
   Ratner on Russian Imperialism and Misreading
   The Brothers Karamazov   123
   AUSTIN RATNER

Conclusion   127

Epilogue   *132*
Editor and Contributors   *134*
Index   *137*

Acknowledgments

I wish to thank my parents who taught me to search for truth. They understood what it meant to be honest, to have integrity, and to stand up for principles that are the foundation of our democracy.

Their gift, which I have passed down to my children, Karyne C. Akhtar, Esq. and Ann-Kathryn So, Esq. offers me a great deal of comfort as they pass on these same ideals to my grandchildren Ayla, Chris, Isabel, and Olivia.

Others who deserve a great deal of thanks include the authors who contributed to this publication. They supported my efforts to look at all angles of my initial observations with a curious eye as they thoughtfully considered and wrote about various aspects of leadership in Russia and the United States. They include Harry S. Gill, M.D., Robert Gordon, Ph.D., Jana Javakhishvili, Ph.D., Peter W. Petschauer, Ph.D., Austin Ratner, M.D., Vamik Volkan, and Nydia Pieczanski, M.D.

The two people I asked to write endorsements for this book, Kevin Volkan, Ph.D., and Brent Willock, Ph.D., also deserve credit for supporting my efforts to edit a book with many stories.

Barbara Richter, a talented researcher, writer, and editor deserves a great deal of credit for her wise counsel and assistance.

I would also like to thank Susannah Frearson, my Routledge publisher, for her trust in my ability to write about various ways of thinking as they relate to political leadership in disparate countries with very different cultural roots.

I am grateful to Jeffrey Sacks, John Mearsheimer, and Sy Hersh for exposing me to alternate views of looking at and assessing the myopic views of many who purport to know the right way to view truth.

Last but not least, I would like to thank my husband, Gary, who helped me see a wide array of perspectives related to political philosophy and cultural perspectives.

Preface

The USSR and its Major Leaders

Although it would be an impossible task in a book of this type to thoroughly review Russian history, a brief description of the former Soviet Union is included to help readers who may not be familiar with the structure of the USSR to understand the complex nature of what emerged prior to the Putin presidencies.

During The Red Terror, a time when the Bolsheviks put together a secret police they called Cheka, mass executions of people who supported the czar took place. Following that period, in 1922, after the Romanov Empire was overthrown, the Marxist-Communist state was formed and became one of the most powerful countries in the world, consisting of 15 republics.

From 1917 to 1924, Vladimir Lenin served as the head of the government of Soviet Russia. During the years between 1922 and 1924, the name of Russia was changed to the Soviet Union, and Lenin remained in charge until he died, in 1924. Thereafter, Joseph Stalin took over, and ruled by terrorizing citizens in the newly formed country. Nevertheless, for various reasons, an overwhelming majority of Russian people who responded to a 2019 poll indicated they thought he did a good job for Russia. Some 70 percent of those polled saw his role as positive, despite Stalin's having killed an estimated 40 million to 60 million of his own citizens. That level of support reached mythic proportions (Gordon, 2023).

In spite of Stalin's brutal leadership style, he led the Soviet Union from 1924 until he died, in 1953, taking the country from an agrarian state to an industrial and military country that wielded a great deal of power. In addition to making the USSR a superpower, after his Five-Year Plan was implemented, he concentrated on the build-up of armament and military power.

After Lenin's death, a high-ranking member of the communist party, Nikita Khrushchev, who was the party's secretary from 1953 to 1958, took over. Thereafter, he became Premier in 1958. Initially, on the domestic front, he was probably best remembered for reducing repression in the USSR.

However, when relations with China deteriorated and food shortages emerged throughout Russia, Khrushchev was removed by his own party in 1964. In spite his ousting, he did many positive things for the people, particularly when comparing him to Stalin and his oppressive leadership.

Khruschev's tenure was followed by that of Leonid Brezhnev, who focused on improving relations with the West, but who was tougher at home. He changed some of Khrushchev's attempts to ease the repression that followed Stalin's reign of terror. While these leaders had some things in common, they also had differences. For example, Khrushchev was impulsive. Brezhnev, on the other hand, was more focused on consulting and collaborating with other members of the party. He didn't make abrupt decisions and was reported to care more about loyalty than job performance. When other members of the group showed dissatisfaction with him and wanted to oust him, Brezhnev didn't remove them from the party. Whereas Khrushchev had no problem going around people who opposed him, Brezhnev was conciliatory. He also wanted to ease tensions with the West, and was in favor of limiting nuclear arms, which made relationships with the West much better.

After Brezhnev died, Mikhail Gorbachev took over the leadership role in the USSR from 1985–1991. He was a politician, who had been a longtime member of the party, and was known as a peacemaker. His idea to restructure the economy in the USSR was called *Perestroika* (a "reconstruction" of the country's economic and political policies). This plan combined communism with capitalism and was led by the Politburo (a group that served as an executive committee of the communist party). While the plan was slowly helping the Russian people, Gorbachev had a long "row to hoe" after the depression of the 1970s and 1980s. This was a time when long bread lines were common, which was partly due to the major divide between the wealthy Politburo and the average Soviet citizen, who frequently did not have adequate food or clothing.

Gorbachev's reforms may have hastened the collapse of the Soviet Union; by loosening controls on individuals, he indirectly encouraged people in Soviet satellite states to undertake their own independence movements. By the time the Berlin Wall fell, the Soviet Union was "coming apart at the seams" (Medvedev, 1979).

Following an attempted coup by communist hard-liners, Gorbachev was ousted in 1991. After Gorbachev left office, Boris Yeltsin became President in June of 1991. He was disliked by the power forces in Russia but was the first person to be elected through a democratic process by the Russian people. For a time, he was the most powerful person in Russia, but his popularity was short-lived because his attempts at reforming the Russian economy failed.

Under Yeltsin the Soviet economy quickly collapsed, with DGP falling more than 50 percent and living standards reflecting that situation. Social services deteriorated for the masses even as a small group of oligarchs enriched themselves by seizing control of state-owned resources (McDonald, 2022).

Meanwhile, while various people were heading up the government of the USSR, Vladimir Putin was in the KGB learning how to be a spy and an assassin, as well as learning other sanctioned ways intelligence officers operated in autocracies. KGB, or Komitet Gosudarstvennoy Bezopasnosti, was the nation's Committee for State Security.

Prior to his induction into the group, at age 15, Putin was reported to have walked into a KGB office to try to secure a job but was told they didn't accept people who "applied" for jobs. The person with whom he spoke told him he needed to go to school or the military before he could be considered. While this wasn't said explicitly, the message seemed to be, "Don't call us. If we are interested, we'll contact you."

At that point, he attended law school at Leningrad University. As reported by Phillip Short, in his book *Putin*, which was written over a seven-year period, while Short researched Putin's background, the young law student didn't think he would be called upon. One day, however, when Putin was a 4th year student, he was approached by a stranger, who indicated he wanted to speak with him. Putin assumed it was the KGB, and he was correct. He was recruited by the group and entered when he was around 23 years old. "On August 1, 1975, a Friday, Putin entered for the first time the Leningrad Regional Directorate of the KBG, the Big House on Liteiny Prospekt, in his new role as a junior lieutenant" (Short, 2021, p. 67).

Being in the KGB was something he dreamed of for years. As a boy, he read the writings of Marx and Engles, and believed in the goals of communism. Coincidently, on the very day Putin joined the KGB and was preparing to enter a world of spying and sanctioned violence, Brezhnev and 34 other heads of state, including someone from the United States and Canada, was preparing to sign the *Helsinki Final Act*.

Among the ten guiding principles established in the *Helsinki Final Act* was the recognition that assurances of human rights and freedom for individuals are crucial to "security and cooperation among states" (Gilmore, 2020).

Hence, Putin was in a very different mental space when most world leaders were thinking about peace and working on ways to collaborate. Among other tactics he learned that bolstered his ability to be deceptive and spread disinformation, he was taught to lie, "'The biggest thing[s]' that Putin learned during his time in the KGB is 'how to lie,' Barsky said, 'Well, I did too'" (Haltiwanger, 2023). He also more than likely learned in the KGB to kill and poison people. Both within and outside the Soviet Union, its citizens suffered from KGB-sponsored assassinations and kidnappings. Any threat to Soviet dominance and control could result in sudden tragedy (Ratner, 2018).

While other top-level officials from the USSR and then Russia were attempting to sign peace treaties, Putin had been recruited by one of the most prestigious and dangerous intelligence agencies in the world, with the blessing of top-level officials in the Kremlin. He, in essence, appeared to have been "taught" to do what he would later do in Ukraine. When looking through a Western prism, this perspective is difficult to understand.

References

Edwards, L. (2022, June 7). Putin the Marxist-Leninist. *The Heritage Foundation.* www.heritage.org/progressivism/commentary/putin-the-marxist-leninist

A&E Television Networks. (2023, March 20). Soviet Union—countries, Cold War & collapse. *History.com.* www.history.com/topics/european-history/history-of-the-soviet-union

Gilmore, J. (2020, July). On the 45th anniversary of the Helsinki Final Act. Helsinki Final Act. *OSCE.* www.osce.org/files/f/documents/4/a/463629.pdf

Gordon, R. (2023). Measuring the Mental Functioning of Putin, Trump, and Zelensky. In K. Messina (Ed.) *A psychoanalytic study of political leadership in Russia and the United States.* Routledge.

Haltiwanger, J. (2023, February 24). Putin's KGB past is key to grasping what he might do next in his failing Ukraine War, ex-spies say. *Yahoo! News.* https://ca.news.yahoo.com/putins-time-kgb-taught-him-112000733.html

McDonald, K. (2022, August 31). What Mikhail Gorbachev did after the collapse of the Soviet Union, and who replaced him. *inews.co.uk.* https://inews.co.uk/news/world/mikhail-gorbachev-who-after-russian-leaders-collapse-ussr-when-putin-power-1824884

Medvedev, Z. (1979, October 1). Zhores Medvedev, Russia under Brezhnev, NLR I/117, September–October 1979. *New Left Review.* https://newleftreview.org/issues/i117/articles/zhores-medvedev-russia-under-brezhnev

Ratner, P. (2022, April 19). The history of the KGB and its legendary methods. *Big Think.* https://bigthink.com/politics-current-affairs/kgb/

Introduction

In order to understand current developments in Russia, the editor and contributing authors have written about Vladimir Putin and the war in Ukraine from various perspectives. They have also considered ways in which a lack of transparency has affected the dynamic between the US and Russia.

The book describes different methods of analysis, as well as Putin's psychobiography based on available information. Quantitative research, which is used as a methodology employed by social scientists, including researchers who study psychological phenomena, is also included. A view of Russian literature adds a unique facet to this portrayal of Putin, as do the perspectives of an Eastern European psychiatrist.

While the editor and contributors used different approaches when studying the president of Russia and what led to the current war in Ukraine—they also have different views of Putin—by working together in an atmosphere of respect, they have made it possible for all points of view to be heard.

In the first two chapters, Karyne Messina focuses on the quest for truth while stressing the need for evidence with regard to the hypotheses we construct.

She believes when judging world leaders, it is important to assess what we actually *know* about them based on hard evidence and facts. This sometimes can be done by reading what they have written or by interviewing them, if an in-person assessment is possible. Studying documents that illustrate agreements that were made between the United States and Russia, such as the ones that have been kept at the National Security Archives in Washington DC, is also important. Some of these documents can be viewed by anyone interested in more information about what happened between the West and Mikhail Gorbachev—commitments that were passed down to Putin—as the Soviet Union ceased to exist as a country in 1991. They are available at: http://nsarchive.gwu.edu.

We can also learn from experts who have studied the history of a leader's life, including the person's childhood developmental history. Whether or not he or she had to endure trauma at an early age is also important, as is

DOI: 10.4324/9781032637822-1

intergenerational trauma. Such traumas include injurious and harmful encounters that immediate family members could have experienced that have affected the person in question. Other experts who have the ability to assess people from afar, such as Dr. Robert Gordon, who has expertise in forensic psychology, as well as extensive experience in developing and utilizing quantitative research tools, can provide valuable information. In addition, it is useful to learn from people who are familiar with Russian culture. Others who write about Vladimir Putin but have not considered these evaluative measures, may want to give some additional thought to their approaches incorporating such perspective.

The overall communication style of presidents and prime ministers is also something to think about when gathering information. These are significant considerations, since some leaders or former leaders such as Donald Trump and Narendra Modi seem to have a strong wish for others to know about their lives, while Vladimir Putin appears to shun the limelight and is close-mouthed or secretive about his life. Perhaps, his KGB background is instrumental in that reticence.

In the first category, leaders want the world to know whatever they are able to convey in all types of ways; through the media, on television, in various interviews, by doing podcasts, and through their social media accounts, i.e., in any way they can put forth information about themselves to the public. Occasionally, there are others who reveal little about their inner thoughts or how they navigate the world. Information about their personal lives is rarely revealed. This is the case with Vladimir Putin. People know what he wants them to know or what can be gleaned from history and the other techniques mentioned above. Numerous facts about his life are not known to the general public.

The following example illustrates the need for evidence. While it appears that Putin employs splitting and projective identification—unconscious mechanisms of defense—as well as blame-shifting, which is a more conscious process, it is difficult to make these assertions about him. It is also problematic to do this if one isn't intimately familiar with Putin. While we can observe his behavior from afar and form hypotheses, understanding what he actually means is extremely difficult.

In addition, there are other possible defenses he may use that observers from another culture can't know. Chances are that Putin doesn't even know that he may have repressed or "forgotten" memories due to the trauma he most likely had to endure as a child. Freud talked about this phenomenon in his well-regarded article of 1914, "Remembering, Repeating and Work-Though" (Freud, 1914, p. 149). In this paper Freud was talking about repetition compulsions. By this, he meant that one is bound to repeat what hasn't been worked through. People continue to do what they learn very early in life because that's all they know unless new information enters their awareness.

Even experiences that leave no trace of conscious memory can lead to action later in life. A child may not have understood the origins of a particular memory, but the repression of such a memory is indelible and later in life works its way to the surface as a "repeated" memory in the form of acting out (Freud, 1914).

For some people, it is also complicated to gauge why Putin invaded Ukraine in 2022. While many Westerners think the war was unprovoked, other scholars, world-renown economists, investigative reporters, and experts in Eastern European geopolitics believe Putin was provoked, and invaded Ukraine because of commitments the West made to Russian leaders that were not kept, specifically the commitments the George H.W. Bush administration made to Soviet President Mikhail Gorbachev, who was known as a major peacemaker. These exchanges include promises that the North Atlantic Treaty Organization, (NATO) would "not [move] one inch eastward" (National Security Archive).

Experts who believe these commitments were very significant include John Mearsheimer, a highly respected political science professor from the University of Chicago and an expert in foreign policy, as well as Jeffery Sachs, a preeminent scholar, world-renown economist, professor, and director of the Center for Sustainable Development at Columbia University. He also wrote the Foreword in the second edition of *The Dangerous Mind of Donald Trump*, a book that was written by 37 well-known mental health professionals. Vuk Jeremić, the current president of the Center for International Relations and Sustainable Development (CIRSD), is another person who believes Putin was provoked into starting a war in Ukraine. Marlene Laruelle, director and research professor at the Institute for European, Russian and Eurasian Studies (IERES), at the George Washington University in Washington DC, also has similar thoughts about this matter.

While some people disregard these Western promises and say they were never a part of an official agreement, letters of reassurance that NATO would not expand on have been kept, as mentioned earlier, and are available for review at the National Security Archive at the George Washington University in Washington DC. They are also available for review online at http://nsarchive.gwu.edu.

Reference

Freud, S. (1914). 12. *The Standard Edition of the Complete Psychological Works of Sigmund Freud* (pp. 145–156). Standard Edition. https://marcuse.faculty.history.ucsb.edu/classes/201/articles/1914FreudRemembering.pdf

PART 1

Looking Within

Chapter 1

Why the Truth is Essential in a Democracy
Pivoting Toward Evidence

Karyne E. Messina

Speaking from my own personal experience, as a child growing up in the Florida Keys where life seemed magical, "good" people told the truth—most people I knew were in that category—and "bad" people, whose stories I knew about for the most part were from fairy tales when I was very young and from other books as I got older. Some of those characters weren't truthful, they hurt others, and stole peoples' property but they weren't part of my life. I didn't know them. I also didn't yet know that "good" people sometimes do harmful things.

My parents were both in the "good" people category. My mother, Catherine, was serious and a devout Catholic from New England. As far as I know she never told me a lie. She taught me that lying was wrong, which was backed up by my Catholic school education. I took what I learned seriously and believed what I was taught.

My father, Ralph, on the other hand, was a funny guy but was prone to exaggerate, telling people I was working on my master's degree before I graduated from college. That sort of thing was embarrassing but may have contributed to my need to prove that he was right, since my first degree was followed by two more as well as post-doctoral and analytic training. That success notwithstanding, I didn't like the fact that he exaggerated, which is really a nice word for lying.

At the same time, he was still a good guy because I never knew of anything he said or did that harmed anyone. He also was a good father as it related to enhancing my self-esteem. I was most definitely the apple of his eye.

I also learned from both of my parents that no one is perfect, and that included me. They taught me the importance of being honest, which they demonstrated on a regular basis.

One time when a customer at their restaurant left her purse with $8,000 dollars in it (equivalent to approximately $80,000 in today's world) they wrapped the cash up in newspaper—I think to disguise it—and hid it under the counter. After the restaurant closed, they called every motel they knew of and eventually located her. When she returned to retrieve her purse, needless to say she was elated, and my parents were glad they found the rightful owner of that large sum of money. They also illustrated through their interactions with others that forgiveness was an important part of life, something I have tried to emulate.

As the years went by, I was proud to live in a democracy where authorities cared about the people they governed. They told the truth to their constituents in an America that was the best country in the world. As a Democrat, I believed in a just and fair world where liberal ideas were front and center in my mind. My father was a Republican, and we had many debates about the pros and cons of each party and his way and my way of seeing various issues. At that time, both parties consisted of honorable people until Nixon lied about Watergate. Even then, I considered that to be an aberration in our political system. Politicians were still good, honorable people in my world; Nixon was a bad apple in a bushel of Granny Smith fruit.

Nixon admitted as much himself: "I brought myself down," he told David Frost in a videotaped interview. "I have impeached myself by resigning." In the process, he acknowledged that he also "let the American people down" by lying (Naughton, 1977).

In spite of this major blemish on our US report card, my trust in America didn't waiver. I thought I was living in "the land of the free and the home of the brave."

With the ever-optimistic attitude that I got from my mother, I assumed that Nixon was a person who made a mistake. I knew it was a major one, but I thought the country could move on. At that point in my life, I wasn't aware of the egregious things that had happened because of American imperialism such as the My Lai Massacre; how bad the bombing of Hiroshima and Nagasaki had been, what happened to the Abu Ghraib prisoners and a myriad of other lies that Americans have been told because of a hidden wish to control other countries under the guise of promoting democracy.

As far as presidents were concerned, after Watergate, with the exception of Jimmy Carter, they were all Republicans; that is, until Bill Clinton entered the scene. I was going to school, then graduate school followed by my doctoral program. I was generally focused on my family, my work, and living my life. I wasn't overly concerned about politics for several years.

Initially I liked Clinton. He came from humble beginnings but appeared to excel because he was smart. That seemed like an American story and one I liked, that was until the Bill Clinton and Monica Lewinsky scandal emerged, which most definitely caught my attention. I never doubted for a moment that she was telling the truth. I also could never get over the fact that a president of the United States could take such advantage of a young woman and then lie about it.

Another Republican, George W. Bush, followed Clinton under a cloud of controversy about hanging ballot chads. He did seem to redeem himself a little by the way he dealt with 9/11 right after the terrorist attack on the United States, insisting that he needed to stay at the White House versus staying in a bunker due to worries about more attacks. Thereafter, under false pretenses, the US invaded Iraq.

I knew he was not the best president we'd ever had, mainly because of the invasion of Iraq that he led Americans to think was necessary because of "weapons of mass destruction" that never materialized. Later it turned out that the war was really about oil, since Iraq was the largest producer of oil at that time, and the US was among the biggest importers of oil.

Barack Obama was the next president and for me he was like a breath of fresh air. Whatever he may or may not have done during the eight years he was in office, he was a decent human being who cared about America. He passed health care reform, he took an active leadership role on climate change by participating in the United Nations' effort to produce the Paris Agreement, as well as setting environmental standards in many areas; he turned around the US economy, he cut the federal deficit, specifically in the auto industry; he supported same-sex marriages; he gave the Federal Drug Administration the power to regulate tobacco; and did many other things to make people proud to be Americans once again. These actions, of course, didn't do much for some people, particularly racists.

Then Donald Trump entered the political scene. I knew of Trump tangentially from his business dealings in New York and Atlantic City. It would have been hard to miss his flamboyant presence on the East Coast, if one read newspapers or watched the news on television. His razzle-dazzle style was entertaining enough when he appeared on the news announcing the opening of a new hotel or golf course. I didn't watch "The Apprentice" reality TV show but would hear about it from patients. His behavior seemed somewhat mean-spirited, but I didn't spend much time thinking about it until I started to hear about how misogynistic he was to a variety of women. That also got my attention.

As more and more stories came to light, the more deplorable he seemed. When he announced that he was running for president, I was shocked, but I didn't think he was a real contender. It seemed impossible to me, as it did to many Americans. A real estate tycoon with no experience in politics made no sense. Certainly, he couldn't beat former US Senator Hillary Clinton, a seasoned politician and a smart woman with a great deal of experience. While I didn't think Trump would ever be president of the United States, my beloved country, I volunteered for Clinton's campaign and closely followed the news, especially the poll numbers. No one I knew thought Trump could win. Members of the Trump campaign reportedly didn't believe it either. There was one exception in my world who thought he had a shot. Although I didn't know him, Nate Silver, a very smart pollster, had predicted the likelihood that Trump could win. I read what he said every day.

Trump's triumph at the polls should not have come as such a surprise to the liberal electorate, claimed Silver. Polling was specific: the race would be "fairly close and highly uncertain." Mainstream media made the mistake of giving Trump too little chance to win the presidency; yet Silver's own polling model looked beyond the existing bias of a Trump loss (Silver, 2016).

For weeks after Trump won the election, my patients, to a person, cried in disbelief. Men, women, and children couldn't believe what had happened. It was a very disorienting time in the Washington DC Metropolitan area as well as for Democrats around the country.

After the initial shock wore off, I started to write a book about misogyny: *Misogyny, Projective Identification and Mentalization: Psychoanalytic, Social and Institutional Manifestation* (Messina, 2019). Prominently featured in this book was Chapter 5, "Hillary Clinton and the 2016 Presidential Election." I wrote this chapter to try to help myself and other people understand how and why Donald Trump really won. One of the best sources of information came from one of Clinton's friends who volunteered for her campaign. He offered to talk to me.

Based on this interview with a personal friend of Hillary Clinton, her campaign made several key mistakes:

- Not listening to blue-collar workers and pledging to continue Barack Obama's legacy,
- Not realizing the "Black Lives Matter" mantra would be interpreted as "White Lives Don't Matter," and that support of the LGBTQ community might be understood as a position of gay superiority,
- Not incorporating a focused strategy of outreach to the Rust Belt states, nor using Joe Biden—a supporter of the working class—to campaign,
- Not showing Hillary's concern for veterans and their families, nor for the challenges of working mothers,
- Not getting outside the Beltway to understand real-life conditions in the nation's heartland, and
- Not focusing on areas where voters were "sinking" economically, but instead, looking toward the population whose fortunes were rising.

(Messina, 2019)

Eventually, while working on this book, as I was more able to gather my wits about me and begin to think again from a psychoanalytic perspective, I recognized the mechanisms of defense I knew so well: splitting, projective identification, and blame-shifting. Applied to politics these maneuvers were inherent in a "divide and conquer" mindset. If you separate and isolate the "good" from the "bad" people and align yourself with the "good" group, you can identify with their struggles while convincing them you understand their plight in life because you are actually just like them. In the meantime, the "bad" people are said to be worthless elitists who only care about themselves.

The next four years in Washington were hell. Right from the start the lies Trump told were incredulous. How or why did he do this so much, I often asked myself.

As bad as the era of Trump was for America, when it ended, I was able to regain my equilibrium and return to my optimistic way of navigating the world. Even with the Insurrection of January 2021, the worst was over.

Eventually, after writing another book to help myself and others recover, *Aftermath, Healing for the Trump Presidency* (Messina, 2021), I began to feel that Trump's presence was another aberration. I appeared to convince myself that every once in a while someone can slip into any kind of system and dupe people who are looking for someone who can help them improve their way of life. That's what Trump seemed to do for many people who started to follow what he said as if he were a cult leader. That was frightening enough but the lies he told were more than many people in America could tolerate. Starting on the day he was inaugurated, he said it didn't rain but it did. He lied about where a hurricane was predicted to make landfall and even had the erroneous direction falsified on a weather map. It also didn't appear to matter why Trump lied. Whether it was a "white lie" that some people think are a part of everyday life, such as telling someone you *like* what they are wearing when you actually don't think it is becoming, or an egregious lie like suggesting that ingesting a disinfectant can cure COVID-19, Trump didn't seem to care as long as he was getting attention. That's all that appeared to matter (Clark, 2020).

In other words, Trump shouted his beliefs—mistaken, imagined, or delusional—from the rooftops. And he shouted with the conviction that he was right (Calefati, 2020). To make matters worse, apparently a number of people followed Trump's advice, since poison control units across the country were contacted. This seemed to occur because people swallowed Lysol and bleach to safeguard themselves against the virus.

Trump also made things up that caused a member of Congress to receive death threats. One example of this behavior occurred when he said Representative Ilhan Omar supported al Qaeda. When all was said and done, according to the Washington Post Fact Checker, Donald Trump told 30,573 lies or untruths over a four-year period (Kessler, Rizzo, & Kelly, 2021).

That was enough to make the most optimistic person in the world become a Doubting Thomas. Yet, I was still willing to believe that Trump was an anomaly. Joe Biden was president, and life seemed brighter. COVID-19 was still in full swing, and the Insurrection had just occurred, but somehow everything seemed like it could be right in the world again, eventually, even if it took some time. For me, I think the most important factor was that I believed the new president told the American people the truth.

Obviously, that was a throwback to my idyllic days as a child when I thought good people were truthful. Why wouldn't they be? Even if one didn't like what was going on, honesty was what mattered.

To think about the consequences of lying is also an occupational hazard for me. As a psychoanalyst, I have spent many years helping people explore their inner worlds. This included understanding the unconscious defense mechanisms that protect them from being their authentic selves. Lying is one thing that we often explore, mostly as an ego-dystonic feature of their personalities—something people know they do or exhibit but don't like about themselves. We wonder together what leads to their need to be untruthful. There is rarely any judgment on my part unless lying involves harm to children. Other than that, we delve into how it feels to lie, why it seems necessary, what this way of being accomplishes, and whom lying protects. Often it relates to childhood identifications with primary caregivers or difficulties associated with being averse to conflict.[1]

At any rate, my faith in Joe Biden continued. When Russian President Vladimir Putin invaded Ukraine in 2022 I was appalled and worried. I trusted that our president would do whatever he could to help President Zelensky win the war as soon as possible for the people of Ukraine and for the environment.

Then I read an article in *The New York Times* written by Michael Shear and Linda Qui about the lies Biden has told. Much to my surprise and dismay, as it has turned out, Biden has been lying for years.

Until that point in time, when I heard these stories, I defended Biden to the nth degree. I wouldn't accept that he lied. While this may in part have been a reaction to Trump's outrageous presidency that was fraught with white lies, egregious lies, lying for no apparent reason, and lies that hurt and killed Americans during the pandemic, more than anything else I thought Joe Biden was an honest and truthful person.

According to Shear and Qui Biden apparently said he was a major civil rights activist, which turned out not to be true; he claimed to have three college degrees when he actually has two; and he said to a group of Floridians who had lost their houses and other worldly belongings in a hurricane that something very similar had happened to him. What actually occurred in his home was that he once had a small fire in his kitchen, and which was contained.

Thereafter I learned that he had used the words of others and passed them off as his own, not once but several times.

According to *The New York Times*, Joe Biden's history of fabrications had been not just lengthy but highly detailed and well documented: he used part of a "moving" speech by British Labor Party leader Neil Kinnock without attribution, as well as passages from speeches by Robert F. Kennedy and Hubert H. Humphrey; he had been disciplined during law school for plagiarism of a law review article; and he exaggerated his academic accomplishments (Shear & Qui, 2022).

Call it storytelling, exaggeration, or anything else that skirts the truth, it appears that Joe Biden has been lying to the American public for decades. Although I didn't want to believe it, the more the fog was lifted from my mind, the more I realized I had heard what I wanted to hear, not what was true, such as the fact that he was forced to withdraw from the 1987 presidential race because of plagiarism. While I wasn't tuned into politics at the time, I think one-time candidate Gary Hart's affair that caused him to be the first candidate to drop out of that race must have prevented me unconsciously from focusing on Biden. I also wasn't interested in his candidacy at that point in time because I was supporting Hart.

Upon reflection, I think like many Americans who were so thrown off by Donald Trump's incessant inability to be truthful, I lost my ability to consider anything negative about Joe Biden. For that I think we all get a pass. It was truly an awful four years of our lives when Trump was in the White House, along with a very scary virus that killed over 400,000 people in the US while he was president. However, the material about Biden was available for years if I had been able to hear the truth. After I was more able to face facts, I wanted to know more so I kept reading.

Liz Peek, the Opinion Contributor at *The Hill*, reviewed Biden's record in detail and the picture was much bleaker than I thought. According to Ms. Peek, "In fact, Biden has a long history of lying—about himself, about his past and about events that never took place" (Peek, 2020).

Much to my chagrin, Biden claimed he went to law school on a full scholarship and was at the top of his class. Instead, he received a partial scholarship based on financial need and graduated 76th out of a class of 86 students. He also said that he was nearly arrested for trying to visit Nelson Mandela when Mandela was in prison. Apparently, that didn't happen. While Biden went with a delegation to South Africa, he got separated from the group of people with whom he was traveling, and no one arrested him.

Liz Peek also reminded me of something, which as a psychoanalyst I'd known for years but didn't want to face, namely,

> Character does not change. Biden's winning smile and genial nature have granted him license to mislead. But as Biden denies alleged misdeeds related to US National Security Advisor General Michael Flynn, to his own son Hunter's involvement in Ukraine or to Tara Reade, his history of bending the truth is informative.

Reade was a former Biden Senate aide who accused her employer of sexual harassment (Peek, 2022).

This knowledge shifted my outlook on US politicians and led me to start questioning other aspects of what it really meant to trust the statements made by presidents. I wondered what else I believed that wasn't true. This led me to start checking out other things I'd heard in passing over the years that I never seriously questioned because of my focus, which was on my career, my patients, and my family. I was studying psychoanalytic thinking and technique and not the illegal, unethical, and amoral events that happened in many countries around the world that were initiated by the United States.

Examples of these events included what occurred in Japan, Vietnam, and My Lai. Other things that occurred that I started to read about in-depth included the Iran-Contra Affair and the torture that took place at Abu Ghraib.

Time did not permit me to do a thorough review of all of the presidential lies that have been told to the American people but some of the most harmful ones opened my eyes to a major character flaw in many of our presidents, i.e., their propensity to lie.

My search began when I remembered a discussion I had with a friend years earlier who told me we *had* to bomb Hiroshima and Nagasaki. I questioned what he said at the time but put it out of my mind.

Harry Truman's Big Lie and the Aftermath of the Atomic Bomb

Based on that discussion and my interest in reviewing presidential lies, I decided to start with Harry Truman, who made the decision to use nuclear weapons in Japan. During the period before the bombs were dropped on Hiroshima and Nagasaki, it appears as though it was vitally important to the Truman White House that an image of military power be communicated to the American people while at the same time conveying the importance of American values, which included decency and a concern for the lives of others.

Truman carefully crafted a message for general consumption that purposely did not name the target city. Truman also cast the nuclear attack's target as strictly military, rather than a mostly civilian cityscape. Perhaps most notable was Truman's avoidance of describing the potential effects of nuclear radiation; instead he simply said the bomb was "revolutionary" in its destructive power (Mitchell, 2020).

Another reason given for dropping bombs in Japan was to end the war quickly without losing more American lives. That doesn't really make sense since the Japanese military leaders were trying to find a way to end the war. What is more accurate is this information: the US wanted to minimize the number of American troops that could be lost with continued conventional warfare, as well as to assure America's primacy in a new post-war world order (Peace Promotion Division, n.d.).

No matter what Truman wanted to achieve, the cost of human life and the agony and suffering cannot be overlooked. It was a horrendous act of terror that marred the dignity of humanity. This lack of factual data affected the American people a great deal right after the war. According to a Gallup poll in 1945, some 85 percent of Americans approved of the use of the atom bombs in Hiroshima and Nagasaki, but unfortunately Americans hadn't been given accurate information.

In 1991, according to information provided by the *Detroit Free Press*, the percentage had changed to 63 percent and by 2015 the data suggested that only 56 percent of Americans approved of this war. Although there doesn't appear to be any current data about the opinions of US citizens in 2023, it would be interesting to know what percentage of Americans now believe we should have bombed Japan (Moore, 2021).

No matter how the polling has fluctuated over time, President Truman went out of his way to assure doubters like Robert J. Oppenheimer, mastermind of America's atomic bomb, that the president alone held responsibility for any decisions about using the weapon. "You just don't go around bellyaching about it," Truman was to say (Bella, 2023).

Another person who knows about the devastation that is caused by nuclear weapons is James Merikangas, a distinguished neurologist who was a nuclear weapon loading officer after graduating from the US Navy Guided Missile School. He said, "As World War I turned out to not be 'the war to end all wars,' the denouement of World War II in the Pacific was the beginning of the Atomic Age with the nuclear incineration of Hiroshima and Nagasaki" (Wood, 2023).

In addition, Merikangas also contended that the "good wars" of fighting evil and oppression and invasion "are gone." What has replaced them are heavy civilian casualties and the ashes of cities, and the creation of "psychotic dreams of charismatic tyrants, all in the name of clans, religions, or races."

After witnessing the last above-ground hydrogen bomb tested in the United States from the deck of the *USS Kitty Hawk* on July 9, 1962, Merikangas made the decision "to leave the service and go to medical school, moving from mass destruction to individual healing" (Wood, 2023).

He is obviously a man who knows about the catastrophic results of nuclear warfare. He now writes about the intense anxiety that the world is experiencing because of Putin's threats to use nuclear weapons in Ukraine, which Merikangas believes is unconscionable. Thankfully, he is reminding us about the pernicious effects of the atom bomb in the 1940s and the last above-ground hydrogen bomb test he witnessed, in 1962.

Others have written in detail about what was reported right after the bomb was dropped: Truman's voice "tense with excitement" announcing the "overwhelming success" of the bomb test. However, at least one account left out Truman's "exultant remark" that the test marked "the greatest thing in history!" (Mitchell, 2020).

When all was said and done, was the bombing of Hiroshima and Nagasaki necessary to end the war with Japan? Is this a rationalization that is bandied about by many hardliners who believe Harry Truman's version of how and why World War II ended? Did it save countless American lives, as they claim? Most well-respected historians disagree. They also don't think it changed the minds of the Japanese military. Instead, current thinking suggests that Truman's real motive for using nuclear weapons in Japan was to make sure the United States was more powerful than the Soviet Union.

According to Gar Alperovitz, a historian and scholar who has spent many years researching and discussing this topic, Truman was cut from a courser cloth than the more diplomatic Franklin Roosevelt: bluff and "tough-talking." Truman could see around the corner of post-war relations with the Soviet leadership, and no matter whether it was militarily correct to use nuclear bombs, he wanted the upper hand in drawing the world map once the war ended. Truman intended to influence the balance of power, not be a bystander (Alperovitz, 2022).

Years later, in 2020, an Op-Ed piece written by Alperovitz and Sherwin appeared in the *Los Angeles Times*. This view is also documented on a plaque at the National Museum of the US Navy in Washington DC. According to Alperovitz and Sherwin, the Soviet invasion of Manchuria, not the loss of 135,000 lives in Hiroshima and Nagasaki, was what tipped the scales (Alperovitz & Sherwin, 2020).

They go on to point out that the truth has been again diluted in the online version of the initial statement, "as revision to put the atomic bombings in a more positive light—once again showing how myths can overwhelm historical evidence" (Alperovitz & Sherman, 2020). US military attacks on the Japanese Homes Islands, aimed at Japanese industrial might, were coupled with British naval attacks on Japan's merchant marine. Finally came the direct threat described in the Potsdam Proclamation, which promised "utter destruction" unless Japanese surrender was forthcoming. Then came the atomic bombs, which led to Japan's acceptance of the Potsdam Declaration on August 10, 1945 (National Museum of the US Navy, 2022). Call them myths or call them lies, Truman's motives were not altruistic. Somehow his slant seemed to have affected how Americans thought of this massacre in 1945 and for years that followed the ending of the war. To some extent that mindset still exists in 2023.

Lyndon Johnson and the Maddox Incident

Another most unfortunate lie was told by Lyndon Johnson as it relates to the US destroyer *Maddox*. Believing his ship was under nighttime attack off the North Vietnamese coast on August 4, 1964, the captain later admitted that an "overeager sonarman" had misinterpreted the sound of his own ship's propeller, and that this mistake led to two hours of outgoing fire from the *Maddox* and the nearby *USS Turner Joy* (Smitha, 2014).

Later, in spite of information to the contrary, President Johnson and Secretary of Defense Robert McNamara, kept the story alive. They insisted that the attack happened and went to Congress to seek approval for further escalation. Eventually Johnson's actions led to the Gulf of Tonkin Resolution, which in essence gave him a blank check for the rest of his presidency.

After lying and deceiving Congress and the American people every step of the way, when all was said and done, Johnson escalated America's war in Asia. This travesty cost some 50,000 US military men, as well as 220,000 Saigon military casualties, up to 1 million Communist fighters' lives, and civilian deaths estimated up to 4 million (Smitha, 2014).

President Reagan, Vice-President Bush and the Iran-Contra Affair

It turns out that Ronald Regan lied about sending arms to Iran to release hostages. At that time the US had a strict policy forbidding the government to give in to terrorists' demands. Contradicting evidence that later emerged, Reagan insisted that swapping weapons for American hostages was "utterly false" and against a firm "no-concessions policy." He stated: "We did not—repeat—we did not trade weapons or anything else for hostages" (Hoffman, 1987).

According to an analysis conducted at the University of Pennsylvania, the news about the Iran-Contra Affair stunned both the American and the international public, by and large, because it involved a number of countries around the globe and led to interpretations from a multitude of sources in a number of countries. Confusion and false information spread like wildfire.

However, Reagan didn't carry out this multi-nation scheme alone. He had an accomplice. George H.W. Bush was a participant, but he refused to cooperate with the special counsel appointed to investigate his part in the scandal. Why?

Bush was "fully aware of the Iran arms sale," yet kept possession of an incriminating diary, refused an interview request, and pardoned six Iran-Contra defendants even before a trial took place. Those actions earned opprobrium for alleged misconduct in the perceived coverup (Hasan, 2018).

Sounds like a Trumpian case of obstruction of justice, doesn't it?

Abu Ghraib

While I was aware that terrorists were tortured by waterboarding for the purpose of gathering information about their activities, I was unaware of the details. I didn't know that detainees were subjected to "rectal feeding" and "rectal hydration." I also didn't know that the CIA detained its own people. This information came to light in the long overdue Senate Intelligence Committee report that was presented to Congress in 2014. While it seems clear today that the techniques used could be classified as cruel and unusual punishment, officials in the White House, including President George W. Bush, denied knowing the extent to which the prisoners were tortured. Instead, he repeatedly claimed that the detentions and interrogations were "humane and legal" and that the information they uncovered thwarted terrorism plots and helped capture "senior figures of Al Qaeda" (Mazzetti, 2014).

Unfortunately, it wasn't humane nor was it legal. That was another lie that was a part of the massive cover-up. Twenty years after the fiasco at Abu Ghraib, a number of detainees were interviewed about the torture they received. One was a reporter who shouldn't have been imprisoned. He recalled what he witnessed during the war and the injustice that the people of the country had to endure. He said he was aware that he had no power to do anything about the human rights violations he observed and wasn't surprised when he was arrested. Not wanting to recount what he endured in detail because he doesn't want his children to know the full story, he told a bit of what happened to him and what he witnessed during his two-month imprisonment. The imprisoned Iraqi reporter was reluctant to reveal the troubling extent of his experience; he said he wanted to spare his children the painful details. Nonetheless, he swore to himself never to abandon his efforts to bring the abuses to public awareness (Al-Elaili, 2023).

My Lai

The tragic story of the My Lai Massacre may be a faint memory in the minds of many people who were old enough to hear about it when it occurred. Many Americans were also too young to remember, and others weren't born. However, parts of what happened during that time in our history and the cover-up that followed are important to recount, especially–since the war in Vietnam ended so badly and accomplished little.

The description provided by Seymour Hersh, who won a Pulitzer Prize for his accounting of My Lai, is worth reading in some detail, especially one that was written only a few years after the massacre.

Hersh tells how 100 US officers and soldiers were dropped into the hamlet known as "My Lai 4" expecting to encounter Vietcong forces. Instead, they found "women, children, and old men" going about their morning routines. These civilians were murdered, shot randomly near their homes. Some were "rounded up in small groups … others were flung into a drainage ditch" and killed. Girls and women were raped and then murdered … livestock destroyed, water sources "fouled," and houses burned. The chaotic scene violated the rules of war and the Geneva Convention.

Later testimony established that the hamlet's drainage ditches were heaped with the bodies of slain residents, "almost completely filled with bodies" (Hersh, 1972). We might not know about the My Lai Massacre if it hadn't been for a soldier—Ronald Ridenhour—and a reporter—Seymour Hersh. While 15 or 16 military personnel were brought up on charges, William L. Calley, Jr., a 26-year-old first lieutenant was the only person charged with the murder of 109 Vietnamese civilians. He was subsequently pardoned.

The cover-up by the US Army, the failure of the military courts and the Nixon administration to bring the penetrators to justice are sad commentaries on our country's quest for freedom and justice for all. It feels as though it left an indelible mark on the soul of America that hasn't disappeared with the passage of time. Historians later concluded that President Nixon "was behind the attempt to sabotage the My Lai trials and cover-up what was becoming a public-relations disaster for his administration" (Shear & Qui, 2022).

Forgiveness, Forgetting and Acknowledgment: Can We Move Forward Without Considering These Ideas and What They Mean to America?

Can we forget about what has happened in our country and replicate a time in our history when the ideals of democracy seemed more in line with what our Founding Fathers had in mind when they envisioned the America we inherited? I don't think that is possible without acknowledging that damage has been done to many people. That would mean that in order to forgive we can't forget what has been done but must acknowledge our mistakes and contemptible behavior before we can move on.

After reading and accepting that Joe Biden is not the president I thought I voted for because of all of the lies he has told, I was disappointed. While I realize that presidents are people too, just like the rest of us, I started to wonder if they should be held to a higher standard. Perhaps it is unrealistic to expect them to never lie about anything but never lying about things that are important to the American people I believe is a different matter. Most of them probably lie to look better because they struggle with wanting to be liked and accepted and want to be thought of as special, maybe even heroic. Others appear to want praise and accolades that may not have been earned, so they make things up they have done or accomplished in order to get approval. In another category, others appear to lie for reasons that aren't apparent to outsiders. Unless these presidents are psychologically minded, they may not know why they lied. If that's the case, we will probably never know why they didn't tell the American people the truth. There are also presidents who appear to lie knowing people will be hurt by their words and actions.

While blatant lies that harm people should not be tolerated, perhaps what needs to be assessed by the *people*, not by presidents, is whether telling white lies matters or, as an alternative, should we expect more from our leaders. Should we expect the truth from them about facts when our national security is not at stake, when they *can* tell us the truth without jeopardizing our well-being as a nation? Is it acceptable for them to employ more primitive defenses such as denial, which involves not accepting reality or splitting and projective identification, unconscious mechanisms of defense which are described in detail in Chapter 2?

We expect other professionals not to lie to us, such as doctors, dentists, nurses, financial advisors, architects, stockbrokers, and therapists, to name only a few people we hope to tell us the truth. Should we expect presidents to meet the same standards? While lying may be a human weakness, it is also a problem because presidents of the United States are admired and sometimes adulated by people throughout the world. They are also looked up to by our children who often want to be like them. The example they set is important. Telling the truth also builds trust. If we can't trust the president of the United States, then what? What happens in a democracy if we don't trust our leaders?[2]

According to recent research findings about lying, the previous assumption that people lie a lot is not necessarily true. According to Timothy Levine, a distinguished professor at the University of Alabama at Birmingham, except for a few pathological liars, most people tell the truth.

Levine concluded that there are relatively few "pathological liars," a groundbreaking statement implying that most communication is "probably safer than you think it is." Such habitual liars may constitute only 1 percent of all people but may be responsible for "telling more than 15 lies per day, day in day out" (Thomason, 2021).

A Lesson from Rwanda

There are lessons that Americans can learn from the reconciliation in Rwanda that followed the 1994 genocide when over 800,000 people were killed in 100 days.

As horrific as the loss of life was—entire families were murdered by former friends, babies and children were not spared, and many women were mercilessly raped—when the genocide was over, under the leadership of Paul Kagame, people came together to work for the purpose of achieving common goals; a process that is called *umuganda* in Rwanda.

Whether a Tutsi or Hutu, everyone participated even if a person to the left or right murdered a family member. Surmounting such carnage required as a guiding principle the "public recognition of hard truths." Rwanda was used as a model for moving forward in peace the South African Commission on Truth and Reconciliation, as promulgated by Nelson Mandela and Desmond Tutu. All Rwandans, Hutu and Tutsi alike, were forgiven once they "owned up to what they did." This step was essential for "genuine buy-in to put an end to major conflicts" (Messina, 2019, p. 124).

As memories of the warring years recede into the past, the reunited peoples of Rwanda are embracing the overarching ideal of "Rwandan-ness" (Tumwebaze, 2015; Messina, 2019, p. 124).

The Rwandan "recognition of hard truths" (Sebaranzi & Mullane, 2009), which was an adaptation of the Truth and Reconciliation design formulated by Desmond Tutu and Nelson Mandela for South Africa, is a remarkable testament to what is possible if people face up to what they have done. Through honest discussions about offenses people have committed, a real dialogue can take place which can create a path toward healing. Without acknowledgment, progress cannot be made. Instead, people are destined to repeat mistakes of the past in one way or the other.

Why Truthful Words Matter

Shortly after the Insurrection against the US Capitol on January 6, 2021, leaders from around the world met under the auspices of the Australian Asian Leadership Institute. They talked about what had occurred in the United States in what I imagine was an atmosphere of shock and dismay. One thing that was the focus of the discussions revolved around the consequences that can emerge when a leader fails to tell the truth. Though there is no way their original agenda could have included what happened in America on January 6, 2021, the event may have added another dimension to their discussions since this particular conference concentrated on the special responsibility that people in leadership roles have. Participants talked about the idea that as a leader there's no place for lies of any kind: Truthfulness is a job requirement. There's no opportunity to stay on the fence of ambiguity for very long.

What the group came away with was how imperative it is for leaders to be truthful. When lies emerge, it is incumbent on those in charge to assess the damage that has been done.

Leadership requires the understanding that "what you say matters." Leaders provide direction, answers to questions, and new ways to move past problems for the common good. "To tell the truth requires two qualities, courage, and respect," according to Mark Wagner. "Truth may not be what people want to hear but it's what people need to hear and it's the Leader's duty to provide them with what they need" (Wagner, 2021).

Epistemic Trust

Epistemic trust (ET) is often associated with Peter Fonagy and his colleagues at the Anna Freud Center in London. This term refers to an individual's ability and willingness to take in new information from another person while believing it is reliable and trustworthy.

> [ET] describes the willingness to accept new information from another person as trustworthy, generalizable, and relevant. It has been recently proposed that a pervasive failure to establish epistemic trust may underpin personality disorders. Although the introduction of the concept of ET has been inspiring to clinicians and is already impacting the field, the idea that there may be individual differences in ET has yet to be operationalized and tested empirically.
>
> (Schroeder et al., 2018)

In other words, at any age epistemic trust or a person's ability to believe information learned from others, also involves epistemic vigilance, an inclination to doubt or mistrust what one hears. The latter state can protect a person from indiscriminately accepting new information heard from others. When this doubt is relaxed, one can believe in what he or she is being told.

This doesn't mean one is taught to trust everyone. Rather, it means there are qualities that foster trust in some people. As I've said in an earlier publication, this capacity requires a secure attachment early in life, permitting the child to learn cues from the nearby environment. It comes down to trust. We have to trust the sources of information. When we don't, learning is stifled (Messina, 2019).

And further, trusting digital sources of information is difficult, because they may be shrouded in a veil of anonymity. "The explosion of digital communication and the emergence of 'fake news' have generated urgent concern about a breakdown of trust in legitimate sources of information." This invisible breakdown can corrode healthy social and political discourse (Tandoc, Jenkins, & Craft, 2019; Messina, 2019).

New Considerations for the Acquisition of Knowledge

In the introduction to a book written in 2021, *Virtues, Democracy, and Online Media: Epistemic Issues*, the editors introduce new ways some people are defining truth that is currently fraught with false information, or "post-truth." That phrase indicates not necessarily falsehood, but a massaging of true facts by distortions or "alternative" means of presentation (Snow & Vaccarezza, 2021).

In many cases, since like-minded people gather, share, and post information without challenges, false information is confirmed and reinforced. In this closed system, there aren't dissenting voices, opposing views are not made available. There is little or no exchange of ideas or opportunities to air differences.

Some observers posit that social media is risky for democratic values, and that citizens themselves bear some responsibility for a closed-loop configuration where "facts" are not challenged for verification (Snow & Vaccarezza, 2021).

Perhaps in our complicated world filled with false information and fake news, it will be incumbent on all of us who wish to participate in a democracy to critically evaluate the sources of information we take in. If we enter into a process wherein we assess what is factual information, we hopefully may be able to demand leaders who are there with us engaging in the search for truth without lying to us. Only then will we be able to say we are living in a true democracy.

James Pfiffner, a professor from George Mason University, understands how lying affects democracy, believing we have a responsibility to assess the moral character of our leaders. "The issue of presidential lying," Pfiffner writes, "undercuts the democratic link between citizens and their government." Such "obvious lying" can reinforce later lies that in turn chips away at the concept of moral responsibility in democratic governance (Pfiffner, 1999).

Making a Case for Evidence: How It Can Help Us Follow the Intentions of Our Founding Fathers

> Any non-skeptical epistemological theory should hold that, if we want to know what the world is like, our best bet is to believe what our evidence supports. Evidence is a guide to truth.
>
> (Eckert, 2022)

This idea supports my major premise: We need evidence to be certain about our hypotheses. Without it what we say and write is highly speculative. With evidence, hopefully we may be able to return to a time when Americans felt they could believe the news, our president, and each other without a cloud of suspicion hanging over us; a time when truthfulness was a given, not an unexpected surprise.

Another way of describing this concept was espoused by the late Christopher Hitchens, a socio-political writer who said, "What can be asserted without evidence can be dismissed without evidence." This idea became known as Hitchens' razor, a maxim holding that one who makes a claim must support that claim with evidence, rather than expecting an opponent to take up the responsibility to refute it (Peterson, 2021).

If we are to follow the advice of the framers of our Constitution, *evidence* will serve us well since they did not intend for the document that set forth the principles of our democracy to be static, but instead they intended for us to make changes.

In order for the people in the United States "to form [and maintain] a more perfect Union," the framers of our Constitution charged subsequent generations with the task of guarding and protecting and *reevaluating* our needs. We now have an obligation to assess how we went awry and how we can recreate the spirit of democracy that will slip away if we remain divided while letting fake news and false information dominate what we know about our country.

In their wisdom, the framers of the US Constitution designed it to last through generations, establishing principles that were both firm and flexible to take human advances and crises into account (Stone & Marshall, 2011).

A Ray of Light?

In an unexpected development on Tuesday, April 19, 2023, Fox News agreed to pay $787.5 million to resolve a defamation suit filed by Dominion

Voting Systems for making false claims against the company in the 2020 presidential election.

Prior to the announcement a jury was selected and ready for the trial to begin which was slated to last for six weeks. People in the courtroom that was filled to capacity were waiting all day for the first witnesses to be called. Suddenly around 4:00 p.m. EST Judge Eric M. Davis announced that the two parties agreed to settle.

The trial would have been a major embarrassment for the media giant Rupert Murdock, who owns Fox News. Although as part of the deal, the Fox News team does not have to apologize but Dominion Voting Systems, in addition to the major financial payoff,

> ... extracted a difficult admission from Fox News, which acknowledges in a statement that "certain claims" it made about Dominion were false.
>
> "The truth matters. Lies have consequences," Justin Nelson, a lawyer for Dominion, said outside Delaware Superior Court on Tuesday.
>
> (Peters & Robertson, 2023)

Conclusion

If truth and trust go hand in hand, then both concepts are imperative to move forward to make our country a "more perfect union." If we can't trust our partners, our superiors, our friends, and relatives as well as our leaders and presidents, how do we negotiate, find common ground, or compromise? How do we reconcile our differences and repair damaged relationships without trusting those with whom we engage in a myriad of ways?

We also need to be able to put ourselves in the other person's or group's shoes, to understand what is seen by the other that we don't understand. This step is the essence of empathy and is what makes people with opposing viewpoints, often from different cultures, come together and eventually understand each other's way of being.

In a democracy, people in leadership positions often have dissimilar notions about how best to be in charge of various functions, but such leaders must be able to tolerate the ideas of others in order to reach compromises for the benefit of their constituents and communities. This can't be done effectively without having some level of trust in other people with whom we are working.

In the absence of truth, trust can't be built. Without some level of belief in the positive intentions of others, progress can't be made because of the acrimony that exists between the two major political parties in America and among various other countries. Why? In the absence of truth leading to trust, power and greed replace honesty and fair play.

In America, I have come to realize that the ideals our Founding Fathers put forth, whether real or a figment of their collective imagination, have been seriously compromised by the lies we have been told, which is one reason we are so divided as a country. Somehow, we need to work toward truth and reconciliation, but we can only do that if we can find a way to trust each other again, which will require truth-telling and community-building. In our neoliberal world where capitalism reigns, this is a tall order, but I believe it is the only way we can succeed.

The good news is that we are still able to challenge, debate, argue, and write about what we don't like about our country. We can demand that investigations be undertaken to get to the bottom of most situations. This aspect of democracy is precisely why I am able to write about the failings of our presidents, i.e., because Americans in most cases can still demand answers and eventually learn the truth.

Americans are still part of a culture where people can insist on getting to the bottom of issues and problems. While we more than likely rarely know the whole truth, we can continue to probe until we get closer to it. We also have the benefit of investigative reporters who can keep asking questions that are unanswered. That's how we know about Abu Ghraib and My Lai. Cover-ups were unraveled through interviews with people who were there. We also still live in democracy where we can tell the truth, but we must not become complacent. We can't let Fox TV personalities believe one thing and say the opposite to millions of people on the news, as they have recently admitted to doing during and after the January 2021 Insurrection at the US Capitol. We don't need and shouldn't accept Democratic news or Republican news. We need to be able to read or hear the news that accurately represents what has occurred, perhaps without personal commentaries made by newscasters. We the people should still be able to learn the truth about what is occurring in our country and around the world without a biased interpretation from left-leaning or right-leaning sources of information.

Is there a ray of hope? In a late-breaking news story on April 18, 2023, Fox News agreed to settle a defamation suit for $787.5 million with Dominion Voting Systems for an incident that emerged during the 2020 presidential election. It appears that Fox News, in addition to paying one of the largest settlements in the history of the country, had to admit that false claims were made against Dominion. An attorney for the plaintiff said that telling the truth makes a difference, adding that there are consequences one has to pay for lying.

Could this be the start of a new beginning for truth-telling in America? If we pivot toward evidence and telling the truth which builds trust, perhaps we can fortify a democracy that has been weakened by lies, dishonesty, false information, and fake news. If we don't move this this direction, as Timothy Snyder reminds us, there could be dire consequences.

A democratic heritage is not an automatic guarantee of wisdom in governmental affairs, Snyder says, and so Americans must be vigilant to easy answers and must learn from the histories of other nations. "Americans today are no wiser than the Europeans who saw democracy yield to fascism, Nazism, or communism in the twentieth century" (Snyder, 2017).

Whether the first Fox News defeat will make a difference is yet to be seen. So far, the most popular TV personalities on this network haven't changed their hyperbole. However, the Fox News group is facing other lawsuits that may not be settled out of court. If that happens, the false information and fake news Fox spread may become more visible.

Subsequent to the first settlement with Dominion Voting Systems and other lawsuits filed against Fox News, in a surprising move on April 24, 2023, Fox News top executives fired Tucker Carlson, a popular news personality for what appears to be misogyny. While these new developments offer hope, enduring change that can solidify our democracy must include a demand for telling the truth, with major consequences for lying. People who have done egregious things to the American people need to acknowledge their wrong-doing. These are necessary steps we must take if we are able to move forward as a nation. It remains to be seen if "we the people" are up to the task of demanding the criteria that are necessary for real improvements to emerge.

If the truth ever emerges from American corporations such as Fox News, as well as from government officials who lie, and if repair is a real possibility, we can learn a lot from Desmond Tutu and Nelson Mandela, who developed the Truth and Reconciliation plan that reunited the Hutus and the Tutsis in Rwanda.

Notes

1 An exception to ego-dystonic lying is pathological lying which is listed in the DSM V—Revised Edition as it relates to mythomania, a symptom associated with an anti-social personality disorder. In the Psychodynamic Diagnostic Manual, Second Edition (PDM 2) it is connected to deception that is associated with a conduct disorder in childhood.
2 It is curious how many government employees are thoroughly vetted before being hired. For example, many people who have top security clearances at the Department of Energy are given polygraph tests, but presidents of the United States are not. https://nap.nationalacademies.org/read/10420/chapter/13 Perhaps some type of evaluation for a president's fitness for office should be developed to ascertain whether or not potential candidates are capable to telling the truth to the American people.

References

Al-Ejaili, S. (2023, March 22). Iraq War: I was tortured at Abu Ghraib. After 20 years, I'm still seeking justice. *Middle East Eye*. www.middleeasteye.net/opinion/iraq-war-abu-ghraib-tortured-seeking-justice

Alperovitz, G. (2022, September 11). Historian: Gar Alperovitz. *Alpha History.* https://alphahistory.com/coldwar/historian-gar-alperovitz/

Alperovitz, G., & Sherwin, M. (2020, August 5). Opinion: U.S. leaders knew we didn't have to drop atomic bombs on Japan to win the war. we did it anyway. *The Los Angeles Times.*

Bella, T. (2023, July 21). The atomic bombings left Oppenheimer shattered: I have blood on my hands. *The Washington Post.* www.washingtonpost.com/history/2023/07/21/oppenheimer-truman-atomic-bomb-guilt/

Calefati, J. (2020, July 13). Fact-check: Did Trump tell people to drink bleach to kill the coronavirus? *Statesman.* www.statesman.com/story/news/politics/elections/2020/07/13/fact-check-did-trump-tell-people-to-drink-bleach-to-kill-coronavirus/113754708/

Clark, D. (2020, April 24). Trump suggests "injection" of disinfectant to beat coronavirus and "clean" the lungs. *NBC News.* www.nbcnews.com/politics/donald-trump/trump-suggests-injection-disinfectant-beat-coronavirus-clean-lungs-n1191216

Eckert, J. (2022, February 15). Does evidence matter? *Allegra Lab.* https://allegralaboratory.net/does-evidence-matter/

Hasan, M. (2018, December 6). The ignored legacy of George H.W. Bush: War crimes, racism, and obstruction of justice. *The Intercept.* https://theintercept.com/2018/12/01/the-ignored-legacy-of-george-h-w-bush-war-crimes-racism-and-obstruction-of-justice/

Hersh, S. M. (1972, January 15). The massacre at My Lai. *The New Yorker.* www.newyorker.com/magazine/1972/01/22/coverup

Hoffman, D. (1987, July 20). Reagan's 'worst' speech. *The Washington Post.* www.washingtonpost.com/archive/politics/1987/07/20/reagans-worst-speech/af936567-4a8e-4b1e-b7aa-9da4f4ab08c1/

Kessler, G., Rizzo, S., & Kelly, M. (2021, February 10). Analysis: Trump's false or misleading claims total 30,573 over 4 years. *The Washington Post.* www.washingtonpost.com/politics/2021/01/24/trumps-false-or-misleading-claims-total-30573-over-four-years/

Mazzetti, M. (2014, December 9). Panel faults C.I.A. over brutality and deceit in terrorism interrogations. *The New York Times.* www.nytimes.com/2014/12/10/world/senate-intelligence-committee-cia-torture-report.html

Messina, K. (2021). *Aftermath, healing for the Trump presidency.* IPI Press.

Messina, K. (2019) *Misogyny, projective identification and mentalization: Psychoanalytic, social and institutional manifestation.* Routledge.

Mitchell, G. (2020, August 3). The Hiroshima cover-up began in the Nuclear Era's first hours. *The Daily Beast.* www.thedailybeast.com/the-hiroshima-cover-up-began-in-the-nuclear-eras-first-hours

Moore, D. W. (2021, April 11). Majority supports use of the atomic bomb on Japan in WWII. *Gallup.* https://news.gallup.com/poll/17677/majority-supports-use-atomic-bomb-japan-wwii.aspx

National Museum of the US Navy. (n.d.). Bombardment of Japan. www.history.navy.mil/content/history/museums/nmusn/explore/photography/wwii/wwii-pacific/bombardment-japan.html

Naughton, J. (1977, May 5). Nixon, conceding he lied, says "let the American people down," denies any crime on Watergate; "impeached myself"; in TV interview with

Frost former president says motives were political. *The New York Times.* www.nytimes.com/1977/05/05/archives/nixon-conceding-he-lied-says-ilet-the-american-people-down-denies.html

Peace Promotion Division, The City of Hiroshima. (n.d.). Q. Why was the atomic bomb dropped on Hiroshima? [広島市公式ホームページ｜国際平和文化都市]. www.city.hiroshima.lg.jp/site/english/9802.html

Peek, L. (2020, May 22). Lies, damned lies and the truth about Joe Biden. *The Hill.* https://thehill.com/opinion/campaign/499065-lies-damned-lies-and-the-truth-about-joe-biden/

Peterson, E. (2021, October 13). Hitchens' Razor and the burden of proof. Elizabeth J Peterson. https://elizabethjpeterson.com/2021/10/hitchens-razor-and-the-burden-of-proof/

Peters, J., & Robertson, K. (2023, April 19). Dominion–Fox News trial: Fox News settles defamation suit for $787.5 million, Dominion says. *The New York Times.* www.nytimes.com/live/2023/04/18/business/fox-news-dominion-trial-settlement

Pfiffner, J. (1999, December). Presidential lies. *Presidential Studies Quarterly* 29, No. 4. https://pfiffner.gmu.edu/files/pdfs/Articles/Presidential%20Lies,%20PSQ%201999.pdf

Schroder-Pfeifer, P., Talia, A., Volkert, J., & Taubner, S. (2018, December 18). Developing an assessment of Epistemic Trust: A research protocol. *Research in Psychotherapy (Milano).* www.ncbi.nlm.nih.gov/pmc/articles/PMC7451362/

Shear, M., & Qui, L. (2022, October 14). Biden, storyteller in chief, spins yarns that often unravel. *The New York Times.* www.nytimes.com/2022/10/10/us/politics/biden-exaggeration-falsehood.html

Silver, N. (2016, November 11). Why FiveThirtyEight gave Trump a better chance than almost anyone else. *FiveThirtyEight.* https://fivethirtyeight.com/features/why-fivethirtyeight-gave-trump-a-better-chance-than-almost-anyone-else/

Smitha, F. (2014). Vietnam 1968–1975. The Vietnam War, 1968 to 1975. www.fsmitha.com/h2/ch26-3.htm

Sebarenzi, J., & Mullane, L. (2009). *God sleeps in Rwanda: A journey of transformation.* Simon & Schuster.

Snow, N., & Vaccarezza, M. (2021). *Virtues, democracy, and online media: Ethical and epistemic issues.* Routledge Studies in Ethics and Moral Theory. Routledge.

Snyder, T. (2017). *On tyranny: Twenty lessons from the twentieth century.* The Crown Publishing Group.

Stone, G., & Marhsall, W. (2011, Summer). The Framers' Constitution. *Democracy Journal.* https://democracyjournal.org/magazine/21/the-framers-constitution/

Tandoc, E.C., Jenkins, J., & Craft, S. (2019). Fake as a critical incident in news journalism. *Journalism Practice*, 13, 673–689.

Thomason, S. (2021, October 27). New research shows most people are honest—except for a few. *UAB News.* www.uab.edu/news/research/item/12398-new-research-shows-most-people-are-honest-except-for-a-few

Tumwebaze, P. (2015, October 23). Remarkable changes: Rwanda. *The New Times.*

Wagner, W. (2021, January 14). Why leaders need to tell the truth. *The Australasian Leadership Institute.* www.australasianleadershipinstitute.com/blog/Why-leaders-Need-To-Tell-The-Truth-By-Mark-Wager.html

Chapter 2

Observations, Knowledge, and Speculation
What We *Know* and *Don't Know* About Vladimir Putin

Karyne E. Messina

Vladimir Putin may have fired the first shot at Ukraine; however, that action hasn't happened in a vacuum. It is also important to focus on what is *known* about Vladimir Putin versus what people *believe* motivates much of his behavior. This distinction is particularly significant in the case of the Russian president because he keeps much of what he thinks to himself, leaving researchers, psycho-historians, psychologists, psychoanalysts, and other experts who study human behavior with the difficult task of separating fact from fiction.

In no way do I endorse the war in Ukraine or Putin's behavior, but I do not wish to draw conclusions based on insufficient data about his motivations. Rather than asserting *why* he navigates in the world as he does, including why he invaded Ukraine, I can only develop hypotheses about what has occurred in his life, from his childhood to his years as the leader of Russia, by reviewing the limited research that has been done by qualified researchers, by gathering detailed information about his traumatic childhood and making interpretation based on that information, and by studying written material about what has transpired between Western and Russian officials. It is also acceptable to consider the information provided by scholars who have studied Russian literature or are from Eastern Europe and understand the culture. With these kinds of data, I can evaluate results and formulate opinions.

Although aspects of the war in Ukraine are included in this chapter, ultimately, I will focus on Vladimir Putin and how I believe he became the man he is today, a difficult task because it appears that Putin allows people to know only what he wants them to know.

I also believe it is difficult for Westerners, particularly Americans born in the United States, with the exception of the experts mentioned above, to really know Putin because they have not had the same childhood and family experiences. For one thing, he grew up in a place that had been nearly destroyed during the Siege of Leningrad, when the Germans encircled the

DOI: 10.4324/9781032637822-4

city for nearly 900 days and attempted to starve its citizens. During that period more than 800,000 people died, and his mother lost two children as well as her mother and five brothers-in-law. The city also had to form a special patrol force to stop cannibalism, since many people resorted to eating human flesh.

In addition, with all of its imperfections, America is a democracy whereas Russia was a communist country until Putin was 37 years old. Choice and freedom were not concepts he understood from an experiential perspective.

Mechanisms of Defense and Why They Are Important

I write books about the effects of *splitting* and *projective identification* that occur beyond the patient and analyst dyad in the consulting room. One goal for this chapter was to explore how these frequently employed and unconscious processes work when used by Vladimir Putin. Knowledge of how these mechanisms work is critical when attempting to understand how observable behavior can reflect the mind of the president of Russia, particularly since he appears to have designed a life shrouded in secrecy.

The psychoanalytic terms *splitting*, *projective identification*, and *blame-shifting* will appear in various places, so, even if some readers are familiar with them, indulge me in a few sentences here where I will define them for the purposes of this book.

Splitting and projective identification are two related psychoanalytic concepts often discussed together because they are both unconscious processes involving the separation of certain aspects of the self and their projection onto others.

Splitting refers to the tendency to categorize people and experiences as all-good or all-bad, without recognizing the nuances and complexity of human experience. This tendency can lead to black-and-white thinking and a failure to integrate conflicting feelings and experiences. For example, a person who engages in splitting might view someone as either completely good or completely bad, without acknowledging that the person may have both positive and negative qualities.

Projective identification, as mentioned earlier, refers to the unconscious process by which a person attributes his or her own unacknowledged feelings, thoughts, or impulses to another person and then treats the other as if he or she embodies these unacceptable qualities.

Together, splitting and projective identification create complex interpersonal dynamics that can be difficult to unravel. For example, a person who engages in splitting and projective identification might see his or her therapist as either perfect or completely flawed, depending on whether he or she is projecting positive or negative qualities onto the therapist. This can create challenges for the therapeutic relationship and can make it difficult for the person to fully explore and integrate their feelings and experiences.

The phrase *blame-shifting* also appears in this book, which is a conscious, manipulative ploy that allows people to shirk responsibility for their behavior while attributing it to others. Blame-shifting is a mental maneuver that leads a person to try to avoid personal responsibility for a mistake, problem, or negative outcome by placing the blame on someone or something else. This practice can involve shifting the focus away from oneself and onto another person, group, or circumstance.

As a conscious ploy, blame-shifting can take various forms, such as denying one's own role in a situation, making excuses, rationalizing, or deflecting responsibility onto others. For example, a person who has performed poorly in a work project might blame his or her colleagues for not providing enough support, rather than acknowledging his or her own shortcomings or mistakes.

These behaviors can occur in all types of relationships—personal, professional, and political: In my book *Resurgence of Global Populism: A Psychoanalytic Study of Blame-Shifting and the Corruption of Democracy* (Messina, 2022), I discuss how splitting, blame-shifting, and projective identification enable populist leaders whose backgrounds are transparent to employ these defense mechanisms to manipulate and control their governments and citizens. In nearly every case, it is likely that these behaviors originate from an unconscious sense of disdain or self-loathing.

While I *believe* these mechanisms apply to Vladimir Putin and are important elements of his defensive structure, I think careful attention must be paid to what is *actually known* about this man and not conflate opinion with facts.

As described in Chapter 1, I believe it is imperative to have evidence for the claims we make about Putin or any other world leader who comes from a different culture, particularly one with which we have little or no familiarity.

This point of view is aligned in many ways with the work of Vamik Volkan and Jana Javakhishvili (2022) who have written extensively on the psychological makeup of world leaders. They have developed interesting hypotheses while speculating about the mind of Putin but do not assert they are certain about their findings.

All of the hypotheses explored in this chapter are based on publicly available material. In their article, "Invasion of Ukraine: Observations on Leader-followers Relationships" (which I have been allowed to reprint in its entirety in Chapter 5), Volkan and Javakhishvili confirm that "the authors of this paper never met Putin or any individual who had interactions with this political leader of Russia. We lack the information needed for in-depth analysis of his personality organization" (Volkan & Javakhishvili, 2022).

I must also make the same statement: I have never met Putin or any individual who has had any interactions with him.[1]

Proceeding cautiously and referring to readily available information, they believe one can develop some reasonable assumptions by following a developmental model aligned with psychoanalytic principles.

Whenever possible, the process of evaluating a political persona, according to Volkan and Javakhishvili (2022) should include the following elements:

- A subject's infancy and early childhood, including the mother-and-child relationship,
- A subject's unconscious fantasies and those of the mother or other caretaker,
- Early traumas, developmental arrests, and oedipal struggles,
- An adult subject's internal responses to external events, and attempts to change the environment in response to internal demands, and
- Transformations of identity, mid-life issues, reactions to aging, and the approach to death.

Further, in the psychobiography of a political figure, "it will be imperative for the biographer to have sufficient information about the political culture and conditions surrounding the subject," including ethnic, national, religious, or ideological context (Volkan & Javakhishvili, 2022, p. 192).

Childhood: Putin's Role as a Replacement Child

Volkan and Javakhishvili say it is important to understand a subject's childhood experiences when evaluating the personality structures of a political leader. This is particularly true when direct contact is not possible and publicly available information about the subject is limited or may not be completely trustworthy. While most historical information about Putin is unknown, some facts are available in his autobiography, *First Person* (Putin, 2002). Though one-sided and impossible to verify in its entirety, it does offer a glimpse into Putin's psyche. In it, Putin describes the circumstances of his childhood which appear to have been different from many children who lived in Leningrad after the end of World War II. Though born seven years after the war ended, Putin was raised in a city deeply scarred after being almost destroyed by the Germans.

During the worst part of the war, Putin's mother, Maria Ivanovna Putina, nearly died of starvation and had been left for dead. Maria survived, but she was surrounded by reminders of death, including the loss of her mother, five brothers-in-law, and two children: Albert, who died of whooping cough in infancy, and Viktor, who reportedly died of diphtheria at around the age of two during the siege of the city.

However, there are conflicting stories about Viktor's death. In one version, Putin remembers his parents talking about the authorities who forcibly took

Viktor away because Maria had no way to feed him. In the other version, Putin's mother gave Viktor to two women because she had no food for him (Short, 2022). No matter what actually occurred, the death of a young son during a horrendous period in Russian history must have been devastating for Putin's mother.

Rumors of cannibalism contribute to an even more disturbing wartime portrait of Leningrad. These stories were confirmed in 2004 when city officials opened the police archives. Driven to near-starvation, Leningrad's residents were forced to make horrible decisions, which included eating human flesh.

As is often the case in situations of this type, Putin, as a child and young adult, more than likely never appreciated how bleak things were for his family before he was born—his mother's near-death experience, the near obliteration of his hometown, the death of two older siblings and other relatives as well as the desperation that led to consuming human remains. Perhaps he heard rumors and whispers of these atrocities, but specific stories in post-war Leningrad were not discussed by his parents. Furthermore, even if his parents wanted to talk about it, such talk was rendered *verboten* by the government. Though these traumas occurred before Vladimir was born, this is the environment into which he arrived: a city populated by survivors who endured extreme hardships, including starvation, cold, and disease. Despite these challenges, the people of Leningrad showed resilience and solidarity, both during the war and after. Still, after the siege was broken in 1944, these people were left with deep physical and emotional scars. Many had lost friends and family members, and the city was left in ruins.

Though left with a demolished city, along with devastated survivors, a spirit of resiliency that had helped the residents make it through the siege continued to shape their lives in the years that followed. We lack direct information about Putin's mother's state of mind, but we can easily imagine that she was traumatized and depressed because of her many losses which suggests that young Vladimir could have served as a "replacement child," a vessel of sorts into whom Maria transferred her wishes, hopes, fantasies, and expectations for her dead children. Volkan and Javakhishvili have observed that replacement children "develop personal ego functions to deal with what has been pushed into them." These children may indeed survive without psychopathology. But they may suffer from lingering effects of trauma inflicted upon their parents—not themselves. "The actual memories of the trauma belong to adults; children have no experience with the trauma" (Volkan & Javakhishvili, 2022, pp. 195–196).

Volkan and Javakhishvili also said that Putin could harbor an unconscious rescue fantasy because of his status as a replacement child. They made this determination based on what Putin has actually communicated

> in his open statements and actions, [where he] has linked Russia—as well as the image of the Soviet Union—to the time and place where his family

lived surrounded by the Nazis, [he] experienced many losses and became preoccupied with burials and graveyards ... [They also] describe Putin's role in malignant propaganda that aimed to rescue and protect Russia and its being a special place.

(Volkan & Javakhishvili, 2022, p. 18)

In their article, Volkan and Javakhishvili offer further insight into how malignant propaganda works in a series of steps. The sixth step, they have written, is "creating a societal preoccupation with the large group's psychological borders through an obsession with physical borders, such as Putin's wish to expand present-day Russia's physical borders." The seventh step, then, is to dehumanize the "enemy" through various methods of revenge, including mass killings and other inhumane punishments (Volkan & Javakhishvili, 2022, pp. 33–34).

In addition, Volkan and Javakhishvili say that replacement children can go down one of two paths in an attempt to fulfill the needs of their caretaker who deposited internal parts of another sibling into their minds at or before birth.

Some replacement children become reparative leaders, while others don't fare so well. The roots of psychopathology begin to form in this second group, largely because their most basic needs were not satisfied in childhood. This includes feelings associated with aggression, anxiety, psychic pain, pleasure, as well as basic needs inherent in being a human— hunger, thirst, physical pain, love, and attachment. Children in this group often bully others or exhibit sociopathic tendencies because they were not part of a mother–baby dyad that made it possible for the "alpha function" to emerge. Instead, they were left with "beta" or "bizarre bits that were not metabolized" (Bion, 1962).[2]

While different terms have been used to describe how change in early raw feelings of anxiety and aggression comes about, one most notable description was given by Wilfred Bion (1962). He called this necessary process "containment" and the "alpha function." In the initial early phases of development, aggression in all its forms needs to be transformed and made tolerable and acceptable for infants.

Unfortunately for Putin—and, by proxy, the rest of the world—this did not happen for him. He falls in the second category described by Volkan and Javakhishvili. Living in a rat-infested building with parents who were too traumatized to give a young boy the love and care he needed–might have created a chaotic state of mind. He was burdened with their wartime trauma. With no family members left other than his parents, who were preoccupied with their own trauma, where was the love, kindness, and affection that children must have in order to prosper?

Psychologist Alice Miller addressed this question of trauma in her essay, "The Ignorance or How We Produce the Evil," as she observed that "[c]hildren who are given love, respect, understanding, kindness, and warmth will naturally develop different characteristics from those who experience neglect, contempt, violence, or abuse." These children have no one to whom they can turn for psychic healing. Serial killers and dictators have almost always been victims of extreme cruelty, although they may take pains to deny it. Cruelty, abuse, and neglect can all main children to life and inflict untold suffering on others as a result (Miller, 2022).

The humiliation that was part of their early development is the same kind of treatment they inflict on others because what happened to them occurred during the formative years of early childhood when emotions are encoded in the brain. Although they often can't remember the details of this treatment at will and deny their pain and suffering, there is no way to come to terms with the kinds of torment they endured. "Instead, he will have a limitless craving for scapegoats on whom he can avenge himself for the fears and anxieties of childhood without having to re-experience those fears" (Miller, 2022).

What Vladimir Putin Experienced in Childhood Versus What He Needed, and the Effects of Intergenerational Trauma

While we don't know exactly how his mother's losses affected her son when it was time for him to go to school, we do know Vladimir was treated differently than most children in Leningrad, since his mother taught him at home. He did not attend kindergarten, where children learned about "collective responsibility and the teachers instilled simple precepts of morality ... Even three-year-olds were expected to clean up after lessons, clean tables and, in winter clear away the snow" (Short, 2022, p. 21). When ordinary, structured group activities began for most Russian children, Vladimir was left to his own devices.

According to Putin's own account: "The way a child asserts his identity is completely different ... Growing up there [on the streets] is like living in a jungle" (Short, 2022, p. 25). In addition, his regular companions were not only fellow schoolchildren, but rats, which he reportedly chased with sticks until he encountered one that jumped at him and chased him. In *First Person*, Putin recalled chasing a particularly fat specimen down the hallway of his building. Cornered, the vermin turned on Putin and tried to bite him. Putin fled, terrified, into his parents' communal apartment where he slammed the door in the rat's face. He said the lesson he learned was clear: never put someone's back against the wall because you don't know what they'll do out of desperation (Putin, 2000).

Unfortunately, people become traumatized when they defensively seal off horrific experiences they have gone through and for a myriad of reasons are unable to talk about. Those who live through situations such as the ones described above do not forget these atrocities, nor do their children or grandchildren. Memories do not disappear simply because these things were not discussed (Lehrner & Yehuda, 2018).

When trauma is too overwhelming to be processed, it is communicated unconsciously from parent to child. It lives on in the child as a wordless but visceral intrusion of the past, and in the process trauma is repeated rather than worked through (Hahn, 2020, p. 224). Hannah Hahn's observations of Eastern European immigrants can just as easily be applied to the trauma experienced by survivors and descendants of the Siege of Leningrad. It doesn't just disappear. The trauma is transferred, recognized or not, to the next generation.

At the simplest level, the concept of intergenerational trauma acknowledges that exposure to extremely adverse events affects individuals to such a great extent that their offspring find themselves grappling with their parents' post-traumatic state.

Though horrendous, Putin's childhood opens a window into how and why events in Leningrad, Chechnya, and Ukraine are uncannily similar.

As a hypothesis, the plan to return Chechnya to Russian control appears to be very similar to a wish Putin may have to reunite Ukraine with Russia.

Based on his traumatic childhood and the deprivation he endured, Putin seems to be repeating a form of his earlier experiences which some mental health experts call a *traumatic reenactment*. This is a new term for Freud's *repetition compulsion*, which involves repeating painful physical and emotional experiences again and again. When trauma is not worked through, events of the past are repeated (Freud, 1914, pp. 45–56).

And not just repeated, but repeated in actions that can wound others. Early childhood experiences that were not understood as they occur can fester, as repressed memories work themselves into the patient's adult world, unrecognized and unacknowledged (Freud, 1914).

While life for Putin remained bleak for most of his childhood as negative experiences continued to occur, two positive events more than likely saved him from total failure. One was finding a person who cared about him and helped him realize that he had the potential to be a good student. The other was learning judo, which helped him gain confidence and become a more disciplined person. Unfortunately, these positive additions to his life could not fundamentally change a man who was deeply distrustful and mercurial (Stevens, 2023).

According to Dr. Bruce Perry, a world-renowned researcher and writer about trauma, healthy and positive relationships help traumatized children become healthier adults later in life. However, there is little evidence that Vladimir Putin had the kind of warm, tender, and loving relationships in childhood that would have made a significant difference. Judo and academic mentors were not enough to help.

Perry also believes without this other source of love a person is doomed to a life of sadism directed toward others. Alice Miller expands on this concept, writing that "abused people in power can do serious damage. Hitler, Stalin and Mao Zedung [sic] all suffered years of merciless beatings and other unconscionable abuse in childhood and went on to be responsible for the deaths of millions of people." She concedes that not all children who suffered abuse in the form of withheld love or physical abuse go on to be mass murderers, but that "all abusive dictators and autocrats had a childhood filled with abuse and/or neglect, and not enough love" (Miller, 2022).

An Example of Intergenerational Trauma

Using the Second Chechen War as an example, history and knowledge of the effects of trauma have taught us that Vladimir Putin understands poverty, deprivation, torture, and all the collateral damages that make war an ordeal. In Chechnya, he appeared to repeat what he consciously remembered and perhaps what his unconscious mind *knew* but couldn't recall, since Chechnya objectively resembled the ruins of Leningrad after the siege. Putin leveled cities, rendering people homeless and dooming Chechens to years of pain and anguish. Tents, abandoned trains, damaged warehouses, and abandoned farms provided ad hoc shelters for thousands of refugees. These living quarters were horrific and were most often unfit for human occupancy. For these people, the war did not end. Though their lives were spared, the war effectively extinguished the Chechens' quality of life.

Then there was another war between Russia and Ukraine. Under Ukraine President Volodymyr Zelensky's leadership and the outpouring of international military and humanitarian assistance, the war continues and has created shocking levels of destruction to people, cities, economy, and society.

To make matters worse, though Ukraine has at times made military gains against Russia, we mustn't forget that in recent years, the war hasn't lasted over one or two years. "We are not at the 1-year anniversary of the war as the Western government and media claim. This is the 9-year anniversary of the war. And that makes a big difference" (Sachs, 2023).

Putin will also not stop on the battlefield. He can't. It doesn't appear to be part of his mindset or psychological makeup if one assesses what he has done in the past.

> It's hard to admit, but every day, the chance of a Ukrainian victory moves further away. Kyiv is running out of troops and equipment. The enemy is better prepared and has significant reinforcements at its disposal. It's no surprise, then, that the talk among Western diplomats is of a truce.
>
> (Schlitz, 2023)

Chechnya, Leningrad, and Ukraine

Figure 2.1 Chechnya after the second war.
www.rferl.org/a/the-second-chechen-war-in photos/30185257.html

Figure 2.2 Leningrad after the siege.

Figure 2.3 Residents of Ilovaisk, Ukraine.

Does Putin Believe He is Rebuilding the Russian Empire and How the West Views His Actions?

Some people believe Putin seems to be on a mission to rebuild the Russian Empire. Beauchamp says he has been telling the world about his desire to "reunify" Russia for years (2022). If he has a need to repeat the trauma of the past, why might this be the case? The war in Ukraine seems as though it could be a strategic move to make Russia "whole," as it was for hundreds of years. He seems to have little tolerance for anything less than what he believes is a reunified Russia. Why does this matter to him so much?

One possible reason may be related to his admiration for the eighteenth-century Russian Czar, Peter the Great, which means that Putin's invasion of Ukraine (and, potentially, other countries once part of the Russian Empire), is a reunification effort. Putin may not be easily swayed from his mission. On the other hand, perhaps his attempt at so-called reunification is a mischaracterization of history. It is possible that his efforts to correct historical injustices are "a façade for a traditional war of conquest" (Roth, 2022).

Putin recalls historical events from a strictly pro-Russian viewpoint. Kate Stallard, writes in *The New Statesman* (June 11, 2022) that Peter the Great was "not taking away anything from Sweden but returning land that rightfully belonged to Russia." This appears to be the logic that Putin is employing. He does not believe that Ukraine is a sovereign nation with a right to exist and therefore believes that it should be returned to Russia (Stallard, 2022).

The Influence of the Russian Orthodox Church

There is no doubt that Vladimir Putin is a brutal, authoritarian dictator who is responsible for the deaths of many people, and now he seems to have God on his side since the current head of the Russian Orthodox Christian Church, Patriarch Kirill, blesses his behavior.

It seems clear that we know *what* he is doing but we don't know *why* he is doing it. Is he trying, as he has claimed, to "demilitarize and de-Nazify Ukraine?" His declared aim is to protect people subjected to what he called eight years of bullying and genocide by Ukraine's government (Kirby, 2023). Could Putin be reenacting something from his childhood or more specifically, the experiences of his parents?

Although Putin's father was an atheist, Vladimir was baptized in the Orthodox Christian Church where his mother was a devoted member. Though the Communist government stigmatized religion, confiscated religious property, and harassed practitioners, organized faith was never outlawed, and so we can assume that Putin must have learned the basic tenets of Orthodox Christianity from his mother. Today, he is very close to the head of the Russian Orthodox Christian Church, Patriarch Kirill of Moscow, who approves of the war in Ukraine. However, living in a country that does not have too much exposure to this religion, it is difficult to even speculate about the type of influence this perspective has on Putin.

Another issue related to Putin and the church that is difficult for Westerners to understand is a schism between Russian and Ukrainian religions. The relationship between church and state is very complex with regard to these two countries and predates the current war by many years. According to *The New York Times*, a major problem emerged in 2018 as Ukraine teetered on the brink of the "biggest schism in Christianity in centuries" when it sought to break with the Moscow-based patriarch. Such a break posed a major threat to Russia in potentially removing tens of millions of followers from Moscow's orbit (Higgins, 2018).

At a conference organized by the American Faith Angle Forum, Cyril Hovorun, a former secretary to Patriarch Kirill currently living in exile as a religious professor in Sweden, declared Putin's invasion of Ukraine "a sacred war" (Vardarajan, 2022). He said that Putin has "the mentality of Crusaders, for whom Ukraine is their Jerusalem" (Vardarajan, 2022). Hovorun believes that the war in Ukraine would not have been possible without direct authorization from the church. As the head of the Russian church since

2009, Kirill provided legitimacy to Putin's reelection in 2012 by calling his victory "a miracle of God" (Baczynska, 2012). This war seems to represent just as much a desire by Putin to assert Russian dominance as is the church's mission to expel homosexuals, secularists, and Catholics from Ukraine (Varadarajan, 2022).

The Relationship Between NATO and the Ukrainian Invasion: A Significant Factor

Historian and Princeton University professor Stephen Kotkin has written extensively about Josef Stalin as well as about Putin's politics and policies. He views Putin as a pragmatic leader whose highly effective techniques have allowed him to consolidate and centralize power. In a March 2022 interview with *The New Yorker* editor David Remnick, Kotkin explores the links between the Putin regime and Russian history writ large, as well as Putin's underlying motivations for Russian expansion. As a hypothesis, perhaps this pragmatism was behavior he learned from mirroring the practices of others. There are several factors and individuals that may have influenced Vladimir Putin's leadership style. A few possibilities include his KGB training, mentors such as Soviet statesmen Yuri Andropov and Joseph Stalin, and his personal experiences outlined earlier in this chapter. These experiences may have shaped his leadership style and made him more willing to take risks and make tough decisions.

Further, Putin's leadership style also reflects traditional Russian cultural values such as strength, authority, and patriotism. He has emphasized these values in his speeches and policies and has positioned himself as a strong leader who is committed to protecting Russia's interests, despite great suffering. Suffering and sacrificing for Mother Russia is a deeply held cultural belief among Russian citizens; each generation has its battles to fight, and it is accepted that each generation will endure its share of trials.

Unlike some scholars who believe Putin is marching westward in response to NATO's expansion and blunders on the part of the United States, Kotkin points to historical precedent and Putin's innate sense of manifest destiny:

> Way before NATO existed—in the nineteenth century—Russia looked like this: It had an autocrat. It had repression. It had militarism. It had suspicion of foreigners and the West. This is the Russia we know, and it's not a Russia that arrived yesterday or in the 1990s. It's not a response to the actions of the West.
>
> (Remnick, 2022)

In this sense, Kotkin argues that Putin's actions are merely a representation of long-standing Russian beliefs, taken to their most devastating end.

Is Putin's War in Ukraine a Manifestation of Stalinism? Does Putin Believe He is Burnishing a Soviet Legacy?

These are common Western perspectives. At first blush, it may seem that Putinism is merely an updated autocratic form of Stalinism, but they are distinct ideologies. Stalinism was cloaked in the cult of personality and characterized by totalitarian control and repression of any political opposition and relied on state control of the Russian economy. Putinism is similarly characterized by centralized state power and the suppression of political opposition. Both men surrounded themselves with loyal henchmen, but Putin has chosen to promote inept sycophants to positions of power because, according to Kotkin, this makes Putin feel more secure as the smartest person in the room. Promoting a plumber to the position of Secretary of State also diminishes the power of the Russian government, further solidifying Putin's grasp. This practice is known as "negative selection," according to Kotkin. Authoritarian regimes elevate unqualified people to positions of power because "they won't be too competent, too clever, to organize a coup against them. Putin surrounds himself with people who are maybe not the sharpest tools in the drawer on purpose" (Remnick, 2022).

Kotkin's analysis supports part of one of my hypotheses that, though Putin is engaging in some unconscious forms of projective identification, he is also acutely aware of how others, especially in the West, perceive him. Putin is not crazy, though, as Kotkin points out, "Putin pretends to be crazy in order to scare us and to gain leverage" (Remnick, 2022).

John Mearsheimer, a political science professor from the University of Chicago and an expert in foreign policy, sees it differently. He believes Putin's invasion of Ukraine was brought about by the West. He contends that the United States forced Putin's hand through its promotion of NATO and long-held belief that Putin is the enemy of Ukraine. After Russia annexed Crimea in 2014, Mearsheimer wrote that "the United States and its European allies share most of the responsibility for this crisis" (Mearsheimer, 2014) due in large part to NATO expansion and the EU's growth eastward. Mearsheimer traces how Putin could perceive this movement as a threat as far back as the mid-1990s, when NATO began moving East while Russian leaders were expressing their concerns.

Mearsheimer told Isaac Chotiner that in February 2022 he had initially believed that Putin wanted to reintegrate Ukraine into Russia. By November of that year, Mearsheimer no longer felt that was true. However, he still believed that Putin had no interest in recreating the Soviet Union. "I think there's no question that his goals have escalated since the war started on February 24th, but not to the point where he's interested in conquering all of Ukraine" (Chotiner, 2022a).

Chotiner spoke with Mearsheimer again in March 2022, and Mearsheimer remained steadfast in his belief that the US had pushed Russia to this:

> I think all the trouble ... started in April 2008, at the NATO Summit in Bucharest, where afterward NATO issued a statement that said Ukraine and Georgia would become part of NATO. The Russians made it unequivocally clear at the time that they viewed this as an existential threat ...
> (Chotiner, 2022a)

The truth of Putin's motives exists; however, it is unlikely we will ever understand those motives entirely.

In November 2022, after nine months of the war in Ukraine, *The New Yorker*'s Isaac Chotiner sat down with Mearsheimer to see whether the analyst's feelings on Russia's invasion had evolved. At that time, Mearsheimer felt that the Russians were "behaving more ruthlessly towards the Ukrainians that they were initially" (Chotiner, 2022b). He also indicated that the Russians were employing more brutal tactics, adding that a victory in Ukraine would include conquering and then maintaining control of the four oblasts they had taken possession of while making sure Ukraine was not connected to NATO in any way.

These exchanges bring to mind the Volkan and Javakhishvili paper as it relates to the puzzling behavior of political leaders. They hold that "conventional, rational approaches" may not apply in all domestic or international decision-making. Individual psychologies of decision-makers can become "agitated" by a plethora of external factors in the political environment, not to mention emotional upheavals. By extension, these "agitated" decision-makers may try to re-form the external world to create solutions for a leader's "unconscious needs or wishes" (Volkan et al., 1998).

If we accept Volkan's premise that Putin might be trying to find an external solution for an internal unconscious conflict, we might consider his expansionist wishes as an attempt to resolve the trauma that is to date unresolved. Since Nazis seriously damaged Putin's hometown, could he have an unconscious wish to retaliate? There are hints of this possibility in Putin's February 24, 2022, speech announcing his plan to invade Ukraine, when he asserted that,

> The purpose of this operation is to protect people who, for eight years now, have been facing humiliation and genocide perpetrated by the Kyiv regime. To this end, we will seek to demilitarize and de-Nazify Ukraine, as well as bring to trial those who perpetrated numerous bloody crimes against civilians, including against citizens of the Russian Federation.
> (Putin, 2022)

In a 2023 speech commemorating the 80th anniversary of victory at the Battle of Stalingrad, Putin reiterated this message: "Now, we see that, unfortunately, the ideology of Nazism—this time in its modern guise—is again creating direct threats to our national security, and we are, time and again, forced to resist the aggression of the collective West" (Putin, 2023).

This way of thinking may also be an attempt to fulfill the expectations that were "put into him" as a replacement child (Volkan & Javakhishvili, 2022).

Does the West Have Any Responsibility for the War in Ukraine? A Number of Scholars Who Study Russian Political History Believe the Answer Is "Yes"

Regardless of whether you believe Putin's invasion of Ukraine was unprovoked, there are credible people who will tell you that is incorrect because of conversations that took place at the end of the Cold War, between James Baker, the US Secretary of State, and Soviet leader Mikhail Gorbachev. Not only did Putin understand that Baker had promised in 1990 that NATO would not expand eastward, but Germany's Chancellor Helmut Kohl also indicated that after German reunification, NATO would not move into former Soviet-allied (East German) territory (Wintour, 2022).

Many Western thinkers support the notion that the United States is rescuing Ukraine from Putin's aggression. However, there are other scholars, in addition to Mearsheimer, who believe the West bears some responsibility for the current situation such as Vuk Jeremić, the current president of the Center for International Relations and Sustainable Development (CIRSD). Jeremić has a degree in physics from Cambridge University and a master's degree in public administration and international development from Harvard University's Kennedy School of Government. He was an adviser to the president of Serbia and served as the Minister of Foreign Affairs in Serbia.

In February 2023, Jeremić discussed the complex geopolitics of the Balkan region and how they square with current events in Ukraine, highlighting the importance of understanding a region's history before jumping to conclusions about the war in Ukraine (CIRSD, 2023). I agree that it is essential to understand the complex socio-political history of this or any region in order to better understand Putin's motives more clearly.

Another Russian expert who shares this opinion is Marlene Laruelle who is at the Institute for European, Russian and Eurasian Studies at George Washington University. She places the blame for the war squarely on Putin's shoulders but argues that the "strategic deadlock that preceded it has been co-created by Russia and the West, with misunderstanding on both sides, and responsibilities on both sides" (Burdeau, 2022). Laruelle acknowledges offering anything other than a black-and-white interpretation of who's bad and who's good in this equation often leads to analysts being accused of being Putin sympathizers. Despite these pressures, she remains steadfast that the West set the stage for the war years before Putin was in power and shares the blame for bringing about some of the conditions that led to the war in Ukraine:

> Since the collapse of the communist world, there has been a kind of unipolarity moment and a vision by the US and some of its partners that it would be easy to rebuild a world order where they would be dominating, especially on the European continent.
> (Burdeau, 2022)

The West, Burdeau posited, made a "critical misstep" in characterizing Putin as a perpetual danger and Russia as an eternal enemy. The cultural rebirth of the post-Soviet years was to count as nothing (Burdeau, 2022).

Columbia University professor Jeffery Sachs, a preeminent scholar, world-renown economist, and director of the Center for Sustainable Development at Columbia University, also believes the US bears some blame for Russia's invasion of Ukraine and has stated that the West made a promise to Russia that NATO would not be expanded, but that promise obviously wasn't kept and sanctions served to push Russia into a corner.

However, Sachs has been criticized for his dissenting views and described by the *Wall Street Journal* as one of "Putin's American Cheerleaders" for his contributions to Russian propaganda (Karatnycky, 2023). Like many things I am questioning what we *know* versus what we *believe* to be the case, where is the evidence for this claim?

Whether Sachs, Jeremić, Laruelle, Mearsheimer, and others are correct or not, they are entitled to speak about their opinions even if they run counter to prevailing American sentiment. They should be able to share their views without being labeled as Russian sympathizers.

Documents That are in the National Security Archive at the George Washington University in Washington DC Offer Evidence of Exchanges Between Gorbachev and the West

As early as December 1989, at a Malta summit, George H. W. Bush assured Mikhail Gorbachev that no harm would come to the Soviet Union by taking advantage of what was happening in Eastern Europe with regard to tensions between East and West Germany. At the National Security Archive, which is located at the George Washington University in Washington DC, documents that pertain to the disbanding of the Soviet Union are housed. They contain reassurances on the part of Germany and the US made to Mikhail Gorbachev about NATO.

Alas, the written record suggests that antipathy to Central and Eastern European membership in NATO was baked into decisions made "at the highest levels" in the 1990–1991 era of Soviet breakup (National Security Archive).

James Baker, who was Secretary of State under the George H. W. Bush administration personally assured Mikhail Gorbachev that the West would move, "not one inch" toward Russia. Baker did not indicate that expansion was off the table one time. His infamous "not one inch" promise was made on at least three occasions. He also agreed with Gorbachev when the Soviet leader said expanding NATO wasn't acceptable.

Baker was quite clear when he proclaimed that "if the United States keeps its presence in Germany within the framework of NATO, not an inch of NATO's present military jurisdiction will spread in an eastern direction" (National Security Archive).

This idea was not just part of informal talks among the major players but was written in a number of memoranda of discussions among the Soviet leaders and high-level Western representatives including Hans-Dietrich Genscher, Helmut Kohl, James Baker, Robert Gates, George Bush, François Mitterrand, Margaret Thatcher, John Major, and Manfred Woerner, among others. This "Tutzing formula" made clear in 1990 that German reunification could take place with no eastward expansion by NATO, as Kohl and Gorbachev agreed (National Security Archive).

At a meeting which was held in Washington on May 31, 1990, President Bush himself reassured Gorbachev that the United States had Russia's best interests in mind, adding, "And of course, we have no intention, even in our thoughts, to harm the Soviet Union in any fashion" (Document 21, National Security Archive).

Even Margaret Thatcher, Britain's "Iron Lady," supported giving the Soviet Union "confidence" that discussions about the future of Europe must include their concerns (Document 22, National Security Archive).

What Happened to the Nord Stream Pipeline: Is the West Responsible for Its Destruction?

On February 8, 2023, Pulitzer Prize-winning journalist Seymour Hersh published a piece on Substack revealing a covert military operation that took place in June 2022 that led to the destruction of the Nord Stream pipelines responsible for ferrying natural gas from Russia to Germany. "President Joseph Biden saw the pipelines as a vehicle for Vladimir Putin to weaponize natural gas for his political and territorial ambitions," Hersh wrote, alleging that the US Navy "planted the remotely triggered explosives that, three months later, destroyed three of the four Nord Stream pipelines, according to a source with direct knowledge of the operational pipelines" (Hersh, 2023). The White House has pushed back on Hersh's assertions, calling the story "false and complete fiction," and traditional news outlets have largely ignored the story (Reuters, 2023). Russian media and politicians have praised his reporting (Janowicz, 2023), which unfortunately has been folded into the Russian propaganda machine.

Hersh's reporting relies heavily on a single anonymous source, but that's what he has done for many years, and it has proven to be very fruitful because he doesn't give up his sources. This method was also the way things worked at *The New York Times* for many years, according to Hersh. While this is not the first time Hersh has come under fire for relying on anonymous sources, he's been right many more times than he's been wrong.

A former CIA analyst, Raymond McGovern, joined Danny Haiphong on Haiphong's "Left Lens YouTube" show to talk about what McGovern said to the UN Security Council about the Nord Stream Pipeline. McGovern said Sy Hersh would often reveal a covert operation that everyone would deny, adding that a few months later someone at the agency would admit to it (Haiphong, 2023).

Hersh may have come in for harsh or unfair treatment in his use of unnamed sources who shared controversial information about the pipeline explosions. Perhaps the instructions from the top at *The New York Times* deemed the story somehow not "newsworthy." Or ... perhaps the information was simply too sensitive from a political standpoint (Corbett, 2018).

It is very curious, to say the least, that Hersh is being ignored by many mainstream news outlets, including *The New York Times*, and is being totally dismissed by the White House. Since he uncovered so many major coverups, such as parts of the Watergate scandal, the My Lai Massacre, for which he received a Pulitzer Prize, and the torture of prisoners at Abu Ghraib, to name only a few of America's shameful, aggressive actions Hersh has investigated, this reception seems strange. Have we lost interest in learning the truth about wrongful actions that will most likely have devasting effects on other countries which previously received natural gas from Russia? Do we really not care about what will happen to the environment as a result of this explosion?

At the very least, why wouldn't the Bidden administration want to call for an investigation? If Hersh and several countries who believe the United States is guilty of this act of espionage are wrong, why not set the record straight or alternatively is Hersh right? What would that mean for the US and Joe Biden? Would he be indicted as Former President Trump has been?

There is also the question of why the UN Security Council refused to grant China's request for an investigation in early April of 2023. "A Chinese envoy to the United Nations on Monday expressed regret that a draft resolution to establish a commission to investigate the explosion of the Nord Stream pipelines failed, and he [Geng] urged an objective, impartial investigation into the blast" (Zhang, 2023).

Although China's request was not granted, it appears that members of the Security Council believe that finding out the truth as soon as possible is important so those who are guilty can be brought to justice (Zhang, 2023).

At this point, in the late spring of 2023, whether or not the United States blew up the Nord Stream pipelines is not known, at least to the American public, because we have no evidence (perhaps Seymour Hersh does know but cannot divulge his source). However, it seems important to determine who did destroy them, since Western Europe needs natural gas for heat. If Western Europe cannot get it from Russia, other sources will need to be found.

The Stone Interviews

During a two-year timeframe, award-winning film director Oliver Stone produced a four-part series that included 30 hours of interviews with Vladimir Putin. Stone has said he attempted to portray a side of Putin that he felt American audiences had previously been unwilling to accept, indicating that his goal was to offer viewers the opportunity to see Putin from Putin's perspective.

The documentary features Stone asking Putin a variety of questions regarding politics, international relations, cybersecurity, and Ukraine's internal politics, as well as aspects of his personal life. Stone also queried Putin about his views on the transition of power in Russia.

This documentary has merit yet received a mix of criticism and praise, with some critics accusing Stone of being too lenient on Putin while others praised the filmmaker for providing a unique and insightful look into the life and thoughts of the Russian president.

One critic was James Poniewozik (2017) of *The New York Times* who criticized Stone for being solicitous and "embarrassingly generous." Other negative feedback came from *The Daily Beast* whose reporter described the documentaries, as being like a "wildly irresponsible love letter" to Russia's president (Stern, 2017). *Rolling Stone* found the trailers of the interviews to be disappointing. Instead of hearing "pretty hard-hitting stuff as the autocrat and the filmmaker faced off, Frost-Nixon style … [w]hat we got instead was a series of softballs lobbed lovingly in the direction of one of the most powerful and dangerous men in the world" (Sherer, 2018).

While these interpretations have merit, I felt that perhaps these critics hadn't invested in watching all 30 hours of the documentary. It also occurred to me that those who made these (and similar) statements weren't coming from a position of neutrality; they may have had preconceived ideas of what Putin was like and they weren't going to deviate from their stances no matter what he said. I wondered if they were being like hostile reporters who have interviewed Putin previously. Before embarking on a unique opportunity to speak in an unbiased way with Vladimir Putin (this was prior to the current war in Ukraine), some interviewers took a belligerent stance from the moment they asked their first question. This technique suggests to me that bombastic verbal attacks beget defensive and perhaps curt responses.

As it turned out, many of the people who wrote shallow or glib comments about the Stone documentary wrote their opinions after only watching the first two interviews.

Most of the reviews of Stone's Putin documentary so far have been written after critics saw just the first two hours ... But The Putin interviews do get more critical as the episodes go on. In the second half, Stone pushes Putin on hacking the US election, on the oligarchs, on how long he intends to remain in power.

(Rushe, 2017)

The documentary takes a more nuanced turn in the second half.

Perhaps some of the earlier dismissive comments would have been different if those who reported on half of the series had waited or if they updated their opinions after the series was completed. I'm assuming these people wouldn't write a book review after reading the first half of a book so why would they review a documentary after watching half of it?

Others did not find fault with Stone's efforts. Veteran journalist Robert Scheer built his reputation on covering serious social, political, and cultural issues. He is also known for asking tough questions in his interviews with celebrities and presidents, including Richard Nixon, Ronald Reagan, and Bill Clinton. Currently, Scheer teaches at the University of Southern California-Annenberg School for Communication and Journalism.

Scheer provided the foreword for *Oliver Stone Interviews with Vladimir Putin*, which includes the full transcripts along with additional material. Scheer determined that Stone's exercise was respectful while still probing Putin on pressing matters. Though cordial throughout, their discussions did not appear to be a "walk in the park." On the contrary, both men seemed to be open and questioning in an atmosphere of respect. Even though Putin has done atrocious things during the war with Ukraine, these interviews, conducted a few years prior to the 2022 invasion, appear to illustrate that both men had the capacity to mentalize, at least during that timeframe; mentalize, here, refers to an ability to understand and interpret the emotions and thoughts of others.

Consider this exchange, when Stone was asking Putin about whether he planned to run for president again in 2024. Stone said that he didn't doubt

for one moment your [Putin's] love in serving Russia. It's clear you're a son of Russia and you've done very well by her. I think we all know the price of power, and when we've been in power long enough, we feel people need us. At the same time, we've changed, and we don't even know it sometimes.

(Stone, 2017, loc 3417)

In response, Putin appears to acknowledge the uneasiness that comes with wearing a crown and that unfettered power is "a very dangerous state" and that people who had been in power "who feel they have lost it … it's time for them to go" (Stone, 2017, loc 3417). In the intervening years we have seen this statement challenged by Putin's own actions toward solidifying his grip on power, and during this interview, as I will explore below, Stone probes deeper into why Putin had not followed his own advice and left office.

The central inquiry in the Stone–Putin interviews is how matters devolved to the current state of tension. Thus, they are compelling as a key text for understanding this dangerous time. The intermittent conversations between July 2, 2015, and February 10, 2017, occurred during a period when relations between the world's two most formidable military powers degenerated to a point of hostility not witnessed since the end of the Cold War. And as Stone reminds us in several pointed exchanges, the tendency of power to corrupt rulers of any country in the name of a false patriotism should be of concern in any nation, Russia most definitely included.

During the last two interviews, Stone appeared to put pressure on Putin to address questions he believed hadn't been fully answered in their previous encounters. This exercise included Stone's leaning on Putin to discuss why he had been in power for so long, whether Putin thought he was an essential part of Russian history, and whether his solid grip on power had corrupted his views.

Note that Stone had asked similar questions earlier which Putin seemed willing to answer. Two years later, something was different. Putin seemed tired and less optimistic that his message would be heard. Stone said,

> there is now a weariness that, he makes clear, is borne not so much from assuming his ideas are unappealing to a Western audience, but rather that they simply will not be heard … Putin seemed worn down by the effort to break through to any American leadership.

Putin also seemed to have a strong sense that Stone was risking a lot by releasing the documentary. He asked him if he had ever been beaten to which Stone said he had, Putin replied by saying, "Then it's not going to be anything new, because you're going to suffer for what you are about to do." Stone responded by saying he knew it, but it was worth it.

To my ears, Stone did not attempt to idealize Putin, nor did he accept at face value everything Putin said. Stone also did not reprimand Putin. For example, Stone didn't pounce when Putin made a misogynistic remark about the kind of day he was having, suggesting that a woman's menstrual cycle makes her cranky ("I'm not a woman so I don't have bad days"), but Stone did try to get Putin to say more about a statement that he seemed to sense would be misunderstood (Stern, 2017).

While Stone was criticized for not challenging Putin about these comments, Stone indicated that *changing* Putin wasn't part of his plan, adding that "what he wanted to do was build a rounded portrait of arguably the most fascinating and frightening world leader in a generation. If that is how he thinks, that is what Stone wanted people to know" (Rushe, 2017).

During their last meeting, Stone seemed to be determined to push Putin to complete the series of interviews by getting to the bottom of questions that he thought hadn't been thoroughly answered regarding Putin's 18 years as head of Russia. These questions did not seem to be "embarrassingly generous," as James Poniewozik (2017) suggested or as a "series of softballs lobbed lovingly" at Putin, as J. Scherer claimed in *Rolling Stone*. To me they seemed direct and hard-hitting.

Given the nature of the subject matter and the volatile criticism surrounding it, I believe the only way to understand Stone's work is to watch *The Putin Documentaries* in their entirety or by reading selected excerpts from the third and fourth segments so one can decide independently what Stone was trying to convey and whether or not the reader thinks Putin was being straight-forward.

Regarding my sense of the documentary, after watching it in its entirety, I got the sense that Putin is disappointed about the way the West perceives him. How he would like to be seen is unclear to me, but it appears that he wants to be understood. The Stone interviews with Vladimir Putin are subject to interpretation. One cannot diagnose the president of Russia by watching them, but a trained mental health professional can determine that Putin was not floridly psychotic on a consistent basis in 2017.

One Additional Forgotten Consideration: Who is Talking to the Russian People?

People around the world have been polarized about why the war in Ukraine started, what should happen to Vladimir Putin for the war crimes he has been accused of committing, and a myriad of other topics, but who is thinking about the people in Russia? Is anyone trying to talk to them?

In January of 2022, before the war started, according to Peter Pomerantsev—a Senior Fellow at SNF Agora Institute, Johns Hopkins University, and author of *This is Not Propaganda: Adventures in the War Against Reality*—the Russian people have been overlooked by America and the West. While he lived in Russia and experienced many of the restrictions that are commonplace in authoritarian countries, he believes that average Russian citizens have a complicated relationship with their leaders based on their mindset of needing a strongman to protect them from the West and other enemies.

After all, Russian popular culture seems to be able to integrate two opposites: iconic rulers like Stalin, Peter the Great, and Ivan the Terrible can abuse—even murder—their own people, yet remain adored as father figures (Pomerantsev, 2022).

Pomerantsev also believes a much better job was done during the Cold War stating that, "Margaret Thatcher famously went on Soviet television and skillfully debated and beat their current affairs presenters. Back then Russians were shrouded in censorship, today it is infinitely easier to reach out and engage through social media" (Pomerantsev, 2022).

He recommends that over and beyond political discourse, conversations with everyday Russians should be initiated to ascertain what kind of country they want to have when the war is over (Pomerantsev, 2022).

Again, after the war got underway, little was known by the West about how the Russian people were holding up. In spite of what the West thinks of this war in Ukraine, it is important to consider what the Russian people think. Do we know? While there is a lot of speculation from Westerners, as well as information from credible sources who have lived in Russia, what does the average Russian person think? According to an article published by the Carnegie Endowment for International Peace, these perceptions are quite different than Westerners might think:

- The whole world considers us the enemy,
- Our president is fighting for our existence as a nation,
- Information that doesn't jibe with the official Russian viewpoint is dismissed as unreliable or unbelievable, and
- Many people prefer to get their news from customary Russian media,

And those interpretations go on:

- The Russian public is no longer following events in Ukraine with such fervor, the percentage dropping from 64 percent of respondents to, eventually, less than 40 percent,
- Not as many people look to news of Ukraine first thing upon waking, and
- "The conflict is becoming a distant war," one that may drag on for many months or even years (Kolesnikov & Volkov, 2022).

Conclusion

Vladimir Putin has committed atrocious crimes. Perhaps among the most egregious are associated with his initiation of the war he started in Chechnya and with the invasion of Ukraine. However, with all behavior it is important to ask *why*. Were these random acts of violence that he initiated? *No.* Did he want to acquire countries that once belonged to the Russian Empire? *Maybe.* Is he a psychopath who has no feelings for other human beings? *This is unknown. No one outside of Russia can say with any degree of certainty because Westerners have no direct knowledge about any psychiatric or psychological testing Putin has undergone.* Does Putin have a brain tumor that would account for his behavior? *Unlikely, but no one in the West has any information that can substantiate such a claim.* When one doesn't *know* whether something occurred, he or she can't say with any degree of *certainty* that it happened. That assertion is one of my basic premises in this chapter. People have and will more than likely continue to speculate but Westerners do not *know* about the specific state of Putin's mental state. My other premise is that Vladimir Putin's behavior is influenced by intergenerational trauma that he experienced because of his parents' situation during and after the Siege of Leningrad.

During that horrific time, with all means of transit cut off by the German army, Leningrad's citizens were forced to kill and eat zoo animals. Household pets were eaten next by people who were being intentionally starved to death. Human flesh followed … then came "edibles" like wallpaper paste scraped from walls, leather boiled to make ersatz jelly, grass and weeds, pine needles, tobacco dust. Thousands of people only then may have resorted to cannibalism, as civil authorities "struggle to keep order" with special anti-cannibalism forces (History.com, 2010).

If we don't *know* someone else's culture and don't have familiarity with the way he or she was raised, our ability to understand the person is limited. This is especially true when the subject is extremely secretive or private or is intentionally trying to be elusive.

It is hard to know Putin well because he appears to defend himself intra-psychically by playing his cards close to his chest. Although we can say with certainty that he has done and continues to do terrible things, we do not *know* why.

In terms of the research I have done on Vladimir Putin, I do not believe I have found sufficient evidence to thoroughly assess his personality or provide a diagnosis. This is mainly due to the fact that I have come to realize that being thoroughly familiar with the culture of the person being assessed is an essential part of any evaluation I can do. If other experts believe they have found a way to assess Putin's personality, I respect their opinions.

I also believe that serious investigators who say the war in Ukraine was unprovoked, should at least consider what several well-respected, serious academicians and scholars have said about this assertion (Sachs, Jeremić, Laruelle, and Mearsheimer).

While Putin is fair game for criticism, analysis becomes problematic when the writing and reporting about him in many cases illustrates a sense of *certainty* about his motives when *certainty* is not something and Western writers have at their disposal. This is the case, to a large extent, because Putin is secretive. He doesn't want people to know what he is thinking or doing.

As Philip Short indicates in his book *Putin* (2021), his purpose was not to demonize the man. Short believes the Russian president is more than capable of doing that for himself. Instead, Short's goal was to present the facts, truths, and lies about Vladimir Putin's life gathered over a seven-year period so that readers can judge him for themselves. This is also my goal with the reminder that forming opinions is one way we all navigate in the world. We make decisions based on what we imagine, think, or believe people do or think on a regular basis. However, unless we have *evidence*, we cannot say for sure that we *know* what motivates anyone.

There are also the documents that are located at the National Security Archive, located at the George Washington University in Washington DC that I believe serious investigators should review, http://nsarchive.gwu.edu. They clearly indicate that the West gave Gorbachev many reassurances that NATO was not moving closer to Russia, "not one inch." That obviously didn't happen, as the following countries have joined NATO since those multiple commitments were made:

- 1994: Finland and Sweden join NATO's Partnership for Peace program. The following year they join the European Union, effectively ceasing to be neutral, but remaining militarily nonaligned.
- 1999: Three former Warsaw Pact nations—the Czech Republic, Hungary, and Poland—join NATO.
- 2001: Article 5 in the NATO treaty, which stipulates that an attack on any NATO member is an attack on all, is triggered for the first time after the 9/11 attacks on the United States.
- 2002: The NATO–Russia Council is formed to help NATO members and Russia to work together on security issues.
- 2003: NATO takes command of the International Security Assistance Force in Afghanistan (ISAF).
- 2004: The biggest NATO expansion to date as seven countries become members: Bulgaria, Romania, Slovakia, Slovenia, Estonia, Latvia, and Lithuania. The latter three are the only former Soviet republics to have joined the alliance.
- 2008: NATO countries welcome Ukraine's and Georgia's aspirations to join the alliance, angering Russia. In August, Russia wins a short war with Georgia over the breakaway regions of South Ossetia and Abkhazia, which Moscow recognizes as independent states.
- 2009: Croatia and Albania become NATO members.
- 2011: NATO enforces a no-fly zone over Libya. Sweden takes part with fighter jets on reconnaissance missions.
- 2014: NATO suspends most cooperation with Russia after its annexation of Crimea.
- 2015: NATO ends the ISAF mission in Afghanistan. The alliance remains in Afghanistan to train local security forces until the Taliban takeover in 2021.

- 2017: Montenegro joins NATO.
- 2020: North Macedonia becomes NATO's 30th member.
- 2022: Sweden and Finland explore the possibility of NATO membership after Russia's invasion of Ukraine.

(AP, 2022)

As we move forward one thing is imperative: the major leaders involved in this war must begin to talk to each other directly or through mediators if direct communication is not possible. Perhaps they might give thought to a lesson from history by considering the frequency of communication between John Kennedy and Nikita Khrushchev during the Cuban missile crisis: These men communicated virtually every day.

Notes

1 Permission to reprint the article in this book was provided by Volkan and Javakhishvili in September 2022.
2 Bion and Klein before him talked about the infant's need to be contained. Bion suggested that the baby has sensations of pleasure and pain coming from outside and inside, which the baby cannot cope with alone. Since the baby cannot tolerate these feelings, they have to get rid of them. But where do they go? They go into the mother, so to speak, who modifies and transforms them and gives them back to the baby in a more palatable form. An example would be a screaming infant who cannot soothe her or himself. If held, coddled, and told he or she will be ok, after a time, the baby most often recovers and is able to continue playing or eating or just being. Without the help of the mother or caregiver, the child can become destabilized and unable to function.

References

Baczynska, G. (2012, August 16). Russian church leader rejects criticism over state ties. *Reuters*. https://www.reuters.com/article/russia-pussyriot-kirill/russian-church-leader-rejects-criticism-over-state-ties-idUSL6E8JG2F720120816/

Beauchamp, Z. (2022, February 23). Why is Putin attacking Ukraine? He told us. *Vox*. www.vox.com/policy-and-politics/2022/2/23/22945781/russia-ukraine-putin-speech-transcript-february-22

Burdeau, C. (2022, August 13). Russia expert: West needs to self-reflect on its own responsibility in Ukraine War. *Courthouse News Service*. www.courthousenews.com/russia-expert-west-needs-to-self-reflect-on-its-own-responsibility-in-ukraine-war/

Bion, W. R. (1962). *Learning from Experience*. London: Karnac.

Center for International Relations and Sustainable Development (CIRSD). (2023, February 23). February 2023. CIRSD. www.cirsd.org/en/news/vuk-jeremic-lectures-at-the-diplomatic-academy-in-vienna.

Chotiner, I. (2022a, March 1). Why John Mearsheimer blames the U.S. for the crisis in Ukraine. *The New Yorker*. www.newyorker.com/news/q-and-a/why-john-mearsheimer-blames-the-us-for-the-crisis-in-ukraine

Chotiner, I. (2022b, November 17). John Mearsheimer on Putin's ambitions after nine months of War. *The New Yorker.* www.newyorker.com/news/q-and-a/john-mearsheimer-on-putins-ambitions-after-nine-months-of-war

Corbett, P. (2018, June 30). How the *Times* uses anonymous sources. *The New York Times.* www.nytimes.com/2018/06/14/reader-center/how-the-times-uses-anonymous-sources.html

Freud, S. (1914). 12. *The Standard Edition of the Complete Psychological Works of Sigmund Freud* (pp. 145–156). Standard Edition. https://marcuse.faculty.history.ucsb.edu/classes/201/articles/1914FreudRemembering.pdf

Hahn, H. (2020). *They left it all behind: Trauma, loss, and memory among Eastern European Jewish immigrants and their children.* Rowman & Littlefield.

Haiphong, D. (2023, March 3). Ray McGovern on the truth about Nord Stream, Ukraine, and NATO. www.youtube.com/watch?v=vxX6xat2mDE

Hersh, S. (2023, February 8). How America took out the Nord Stream Pipeline. Substack. https://seymourhersh.substack.com/p/how-america-took-out-the-nord-stream

Higgins, A. (2018, December 31). As Ukraine and Russia battle over orthodoxy, schism looms. *The New York Times.* www.nytimes.com/2018/12/31/world/europe/ukraine-russia-orthodox-church-schism.html

History.com Editors. (2010, February 9). Siege of Leningrad begins. *History.com.* www.history.com/this-day-in-history/siege-of-leningrad-begins

Janowicz, M. (2023, February 9). The claim by a discredited journalist that the US secretly blew up the Nord Stream pipeline is proving a gift to Putin. *Business Insider.* www.businessinsider.com/russia-embraces-hersh-claims-biden-blew-up-nord-stream-2-2023-2

Karatnycky, A. (2023, January 7). Opinion: Putin's American cheerleaders. *The Wall Street Journal.* www.wsj.com/articles/putin-russia-war-ukraine-solovyov-jeffrey-sachs-columbia-university-mark-episkopos-center-national-interest-dimitri-simes-11673017425

Kirby, P. (2023, February 24). Has Putin's war failed and what does Russia want from Ukraine? BBC News. www.bbc.com/news/world-europe-56720589

Kolesnikov, A, and Volkov, D. (2022, September). My country, right or wrong: Russian public opinion on Ukraine. Carnegie Endowment for Peace. https://carnegieendowment.org/files/202209-Volkov_Kolesnikov_War_Opinion1.pdf

Lehrner, L, and Yehuda, R. (2018, September). Intergenerational transmission of trauma effects: putative role of epigenetic mechanisms. *World Psychiatry, 17*(3), 243–257. https://doi.org/10.1002/wps.20568

Messina, K. (2022). *Resurgence of Global Populism: A Psychoanalytic Study of Blame-Shifting and the Corruption of Democracy.*

Mearsheimer, J. J. (2014). Why the Ukraine crisis is the west's fault: The liberal delusions that provoked Putin. *Foreign Affairs, 93*(5), 77–89. www.jstor.org/stable/24483306

Miller, A. (2022, June 20). The ignorance or how we produce the evil. Alice Miller. https://www.alice-miller.com/en/the-ignorance-or-how-we-produce-the-evil/

Pomerantsev, P. (2022, January 22). What the West will never understand about Putin's fascination with Ukraine. *Time.* https://time.com/6140996/putin-ukraine-threats/

Poniewozik, J. (2017, June 9). Oliver Stone's "Putin Interviews": flattery, but little skepticism. *The New York Times.*

Putin, V. (2000). *First person: An astonishing frank self-portrait by Russian's president.* Public Affairs.

Putin, V. (2022, February 24). Address by the President of the Russian Federation [Transcript provided by the Kremlin]. http://en.kremlin.ru/events/president/news/67843

Putin, V. (2023, February 2). Address by the President of the Russian Federation at the gala concert for the 80th anniversary of defeating German Nazi forces in Battle of Stalingrad. [Transcript provided by the Kremlin]. http://en.kremlin.ru/events/president/news/70434

Remnick, D. (2022, March 11). The weakness of the despot. *The New Yorker.* www.newyorker.com/news/q-and-a/stephen-kotkin-putin-russia-ukraine-stalin

Reuters. (2023, February 8). White House says blog post on Nord Stream Explosion "utterly false." Reuters. www.reuters.com/world/us/white-house-says-blog-post-nord-stream-explosion-is-utterly-false-2023-02-08/

Roth, A. (2022, June 10). Putin compares himself to Peter the Great in quest to take back Russian lands. *The Guardian.* www.theguardian.com/world/2022/jun/10/putin-compares-himself-to-peter-the-great-in-quest-to-take-back-russian-lands?ref=upstract.com&curator=upstract.com%29

Rushe, D. (2017, June 12). Oliver Stone on Vladimir Putin: "The Russian people have never been better off." *The Guardian.* www.theguardian.com/tv-and-radio/2017/jun/13/oliver-stone-vladimir-putin-russian-people-never-been-better-off

Sachs, J. (2023, February 28). The ninth anniversary of the Ukraine War. *JDS.* www.jeffsachs.org/newspaper-articles/yjae8gc8hp2p293tmt4dlr4z2dpe2s

Scherer, J. (2018, June 25). 10 most WTF things we learned from Oliver Stone's Putin interviews. *Rolling Stone.* www.rollingstone.com/tv-movies/tv-movie-news/10-most-wtf-things-we-learned-from-oliver-stones-putin-interviews-197547/

Schiltz, C. (2023, February 02). Why it's now almost impossible for Ukraine to win the war. *WorldCrunch.* https://worldcrunch.com/focus/why-ukraine-will-lose-the-war

Short, P. (2022). *Putin.* Henry Holt and Company.

Stallard, K. (2022, June 11). Vladimir the Great. *New Statesman.* www.newstatesman.com/world/europe/ukraine/2022/06/vladimir-putin-the-great

Stern, M. (2017, June 6). "The Putin interviews": Oliver Stone's wildly irresponsible love letter to Vladimir Putin. *The Daily Beast.* https://www.thedailybeast.com/the-putin-interviews-oliver-stones-wildly-irresponsible-love-letter-to-vladimir-putin

Stevens, J.E. (2023, January 18). How Vladimir Putin's childhood is affecting us all. *ACEs Too High.* https://acestoohigh.com/2022/03/02/how-vladimir-putins-childhood-is-affecting-us-all/

Stone, O. (2017). *The Putin Interviews: Oliver Stone Interviews Vladimir Putin* (Showtime Documentary Films). Skyhorse Publishing.

The Associated Press (AP) (2022, May 10). Timeline of NATO expansion since 1949. AP. https://apnews.com/article/russia-ukraine-business-world-war-ii-sweden-finland-240d97572cc783b2c7ff6e7122dd72d2

The Putin Interviews. (2017). *SHO.* www.sho.com/the-putin-interviews.

Varadarajan, T. (2022, December 29). "Opinion: The patriarch behind Vladimir Putin." *The Wall Street Journal*. www.wsj.com/articles/vladimir-putin-the-patriarchs-altar-boy-kirill-russia-ukraine-war-invasion-theology-orthodox-church-11672345937?page=1

Volkan, V., Akhtar, S., Dorn, R.M., Kafka, J.S., Kernberg, O.F., Olsson, P.A., Rogers, R.R., Shanfield, S. (1998). Psychodynamics of leaders and decision-making. *Mind and Human Interaction*, 9, 129–181.

Volkan, V., & Javakhishvili, J.D. (2022). Invasion of Ukraine: Observations on leader-followers relationships. *The American Journal of Psychoanalysis*, 82(2), 189–209. https://doi.org/10.1057/s11231-022-09349-8

Wintour, P. (2022, January 12). Russia's belief in NATO "betrayal"—and why it matters today. *The Guardian*. www.theguardian.com/world/2022/jan/12/russias-belief-in-nato-betrayal-and-why-it-matters-today

Zhang, M. (2023, March 28). Nord Stream blast motion fails at UN. *China Daily Global*. www.chinadaily.com.cn/a/202303/28/WS6422533ba31057c47ebb6f4b.html

PART 2

Understanding Vladimir Putin from an Eastern European Perspective

Chapter 3

Interpreting Vladimir Putin from Afar Leads to Over-Simplification of Very Complex Relationships

Harry Gill

Understanding Putin is extremely important because it is very clear that there are segments of the Russian population from which he has total support. The fateful shooting of Archduke Franz Ferdinand of Austria by a Bosnian Serb, Gavrilo Princip, triggered the onset of the First World War. However, the roots of that war were extremely complex and are now much better understood in all their complexity. Similarly, the war in the Balkans may have been triggered by shootings at barricades in central Croatia in 1991 but the roots ran much deeper. Motivations for the conflict were complex and they included (much like Ukraine) geopolitical, financial, and religious factors. History is still being written about the Balkan War from the 1990s.

The Ukrainian situation is a similar puzzle filled with complex motivations and a multitude of agendas. I will attempt to outline how pedestrian and harmful it can be to simplify a very complex geopolitical dynamic that has existed for many years by making statements such as, "Putin is a crazy sociopath."

The intersection of the intangible emotional connection of Russia to Ukraine as a former territory with the vast natural resources that are of interest to the Western multinational corporations, has exacerbated the situation. The vital need to access the Black Sea, as well as religious hatred that has emerged within Ukraine—including the birth and uninterrupted growth of right-wing groups that had increased violence before the war—must be considered in order to better understand Vladimir Putin's reasoning. European and Russian peoples are familiar with wars and violence, but this remains unfamiliar to Americans. Similarly, some cultures are willing to lay their lives on the line for the ideas and identities to which they are bound.

Justification of Meddling

An interesting psychological phenomenon is that, within our communication patterns, many people assume that "the other" thinks and understands the world just the way "he or she" does. Therefore, we often have an enormous blind spot. This phenomenon can lead us to neglect the support that the Taliban has within the population of Afghanistan. We seem to have thought, or promulgated, the idea that, surely, the Taliban is simply a group of thugs who are in the minority, holding onto power through violence. The West ran into a country, and was immediately on a collision course with the culture and the people, so poorly understood that it led to the spending of $2.3 trillion and 243,000 deaths, including US troops, allied troops, civilians, opposition fighters, aid workers, etc. After 20 years, Afghanistan seems to be exactly as it was before all of the war effort, and the loss of life and resources (Watson Institute International and Public Affairs, 2021). Interestingly, Russians made the same mistake in Afghanistan but decided to pull out after a "mere" ten years of being involved in the war. Similar to our effort, they went into Afghanistan trying to reinforce a pro-Russian government. The Russians took two years to leave Afghanistan (as opposed to the calamitous US withdrawal in a day). The government they supported fell in 1992 at the hands of the mujahideen. Apparently, history teaches us nothing at all.

The Balkan region is an interesting petri dish and emulation of larger countries' problems in a small space with many religions. As we observe the US invasion of Iraq, the similarities to the disintegration of the Balkans post demise of the "strong leader," combined with the poor understanding of the balance of power and religion in Iraq, led to long-term instability of Iraq and the region.

Like Putin, and other communist regimes, including those of Josip Broz Tito, Nicolae Ceausescu, Enver Hoxha, as well as Saddam Hussein, all used unlawful incarceration, torture, and suppression to maintain their power, income, and corrupt totalitarian regimes. As the West looked at these aspects of Saddam's rule, little attention was paid to the internal divisions among Shia and Sunni Muslims. Consequences were dire. Destabilizing an internally regulated system with complex internal forces usually leads to unforeseen consequences when one can't be bothered to fully understand the dynamics before running into a conflict to support one side over the other.

Effects of Fragmentation of the USSR

Russia was a very large and powerful country before the fall of the Berlin Wall, in November 1989. In 1980 that country had a population of approximately 262 million people at a time when the US had a smaller population of 227 million people. In 2022 Russia was a much smaller country, with 144 million people compared to the US with nearly 400 million. These numbers alone support the "paranoia" of Russians, as it is obvious their influence dwindled from a superpower they once were to a nation that is much more vulnerable than the old Soviet Union.

The pride of Russians cannot be adequately emphasized. Unlike many American citizens who are preoccupied with the faults of their country, Russians are very proud of their country, culture, and rich history. It is important to note that their cultural and historic metapsychology very much involves places such as Kyiv and Odessa. The disintegration of "Mother Russia" was a complex narcissistic injury to the nation. Larisa Deriglazova wrote in 2021, in the online Russia File, about the "nostalgia" of the Russian people for the USSR as an entity. This sentiment is not reflected among the 15 independent nations. Each has a very different relationship to Russia but, with the possible exception of Belarus, none has a great deal of interest in contemplating the greatness of the USSR. Deriglazova quotes a study conducted by the Levada Center (an independent polling organization). The results indicated that 60 percent of respondents expressed regret over the end of the USSR while 63 percent believed that the dissolution could have been avoided; 49 percent of those polled named the "destruction of the USSR" among the 20th-century events that evoked in their feelings of shame and sadness; and 75 percent believed that "the Soviet era was the best time in Russia's national history, with a high level of prosperity and opportunities for ordinary citizens." Putin himself is known to have stated that the dissolution of the Soviet Union was the "major geopolitical disaster of the century." If we accept the survey results, he will clearly have the massive backing of the Russian people. Again, this exact pattern of feeling and resulting aggression played out in the Balkans, with Serbs being nostalgic for Yugoslavia while Slovenians and Croats largely felt "good riddance" to the corruption and the totalitarian control of a few.

Much as in the Balkans, older generations mourn the old structure and regime, political leaders interested in establishing a firm "control leadership" romanticize it; younger generations, out of fear and confusion concerning the chaos and unpredictability of democracy and a market economy, nurture an idealized view of the past.

An interesting aspect of the nostalgia for the USSR is that it is not just emotional—and that angle cannot be overstated—it also represents a longing for a social safety net, truly universal health care, free education, a reliable pension system, and family-oriented policies. Note that similar longings are currently very loudly present among the "progressive" arm of the Democratic party in the US. Younger generations are frightened by the world that seems to be careening into chaos (as if the world was not always in some kind of chaos). Climate changes, economic pressures, insecurity of employment, housing, and increasing food shortages can all lead people to long for a "strong leader" who will "organize" the world and create a "structure" that supports family life, health care, long-term safety. Neglected is the loss of freedom of speech, freedom of choice, the flexibility of a career choice, and forced compliance to rules and regulations established by a small number of people in the government. Having grown up through my 21st year of life in the Socialist Federal Republic of Yugoslavia and having witnessed the transition, I feel like a witness to the gains and losses depending on which side of the coin one looks at studies. Indeed, in socialist countries there are certain things that are part of the system: very reasonable guaranteed health care, dental care, disability payments, retirement, a year of pregnancy leave with guaranteed return to work, compensation for leave for taking care of sick children, and housing based on employment and size of the family. We had a secure existence with much joy on the surface. The underbelly of this joy was the total lack of freedom of expression. Expression of national pride would lead to the disappearance of people during the night; all media was curated by a few people in the government and all policies and procedures were government-mandated and regulated. Careers were stunted because one chose an educational path (education was free and merit-based) at the age of 18 and no other options were available after that point in one's life. Once a person finished trade school or obtained a university degree and got a job, that was pretty much it with no other options. Safe, but hardly free and creative.

As I feel may be Putin's fate, former Yugoslav President Josip Broz Tito, who was beloved and idealized during his life, was understood to be a typical leader of a totalitarian regime. However, similar to Putin, Tito was a very strong leader who had the support of the majority of the people, support that had been created and supported through complex media management and culture manipulation as well as the maneuvering of economic stunts.

But let us return to Putin. Many people agree that the unspeakable childhood suffering by young Vladimir created trauma-based reactions. Those reactions included invasions of his country and attacks on his people. Internal reactions based on a need to protect and rescue "his people" against aggressors certainly must be a critical contributor to his attack on Ukraine and his decision to take a firm stand against "the West."

NATO Pushed Too Hard

Based on personal experience, I propose that Putin is an example of a "strong leader," popular in Slavic cultures (I can attest to this as a member of such a culture). Putin is an identified or self-identified protector of Russia and its interests. It may be convenient but also incredibly naive to ignore the danger to "Mother Russia" with ever more aggressive attempts at the encroachment of their ex-territories by NATO. In many ways one can conceive of the conflict trigger being NATO, because it pushed too far, leading to a reaction of a traumatized, narcissistically injured nation and their identified leader, who reacted in the only way that was "reasonable."

Russia has been voicing concerns and complaints regarding the US and NATO not following the NATO/Russia agreement whereby NATO will not pursue any territories east of River Odra (also known as Oder River).

The US and NATO were denying that such an accord ever existed. However, recently declassified documents from the British National Archive revealed that the Russians were correct. The ever-expanding NATO pretty manifestly threatens the Russian domain of influence including Ukraine. One can notice that European countries, being more sensitive to Russian anxiety over NATO were more cautious in reacting.

The sequence of events that brought this aspect of the conflict to the boiling point is very clearly described by J. Hershberg (1995).

In June 2019 Ukrainian President Volodymyr Zelensky met with the leadership of the European Union and NATO. His goal was to reaffirm Kyiv's goal of integrating into both institutions. On March 24, 2021, Zelensky signed *Decree No. 117/2021* approving the strategy of de-occupation and reintegration of the temporarily occupied territory of the Autonomous Republic of Crimea and the city of Sevastopol. This action on the face of it is equivalent to Zelensky's sticking a finger in Putin's eye, much as the Croatian installation of the approximate equivalent fascist checkerboard on the new democratic government flag was a finger in the eye of all Orthodox population who were killed under a nearly identical symbol.

NATO dismissed Russia's complaint of strategic danger to Russia. However, the US was very anxious during the Cuban missile crisis, also known as the October Crisis of 1962, when the proximity of Russian missiles in Cuba installed as a response to the US missile activity in Turkey nearly started a nuclear conflict. Currently the US has missiles in Poland, Turkey, etc., literally at the door of Russia.

Again, Putin is performing his job, which is to protect his people from the threats they have received. It is important to reflect on the fact that as much as we perceive Russia to be a threat, leaders there have similar feelings about NATO. The West has been seen as corrupt and perverse. In the views of many people, generations of people were brainwashed by communist propaganda. This cultural influence doesn't vanish overnight.

The Role of the Split in the Orthodox Church

One cannot ignore the contributions of the schism in the Orthodox Church, with the Ukrainian church refusing to recognize Patriarch Kirill (Putin's ally) as the absolute leader of the Orthodox Church. This schism contributes to the conflict, since the historical forces behind the connective tissue of Eastern Europe can be traced to Orthodoxy. In October 2018, the Ukrainian Orthodox Church officially split from the Russian Patriarchate with the blessing and approval of the Patriarchate of Constantinople after 300 years of reporting to the Patriarch of Russia. Prior to this split, the vast Orthodox population of Ukraine looked at Moscow for guidance and leadership. That split changed everything. One author (Mamo, 2021) suggests that this event possibly triggered the worst crisis in the Orthodox world in the last 1,000 years. In retaliation, the Russian Patriarchate severed connections with the Ukrainian Patriarchate who now was granted autocephaly, a system wherein the church chooses its own head. For Ukraine, this was great news, another step toward separation from Russia. In the Russian Patriarchate, it was a catastrophe. Roughly 12,000 of 36,000 Russian Orthodox parishes were in Ukraine proper, according to an Emerging Europe article from March 2023. The catastrophic financial effect of this separation cannot be overstated.

From a different but very important angle, Kyivan Rus is deemed to be the origin of what is now Russia and as a source of the spread of Christianity from Kyiv to current Russia in medieval times. These are the kinds of root relationships that people are willing to die for. The split was very heated, and Putin and Petro Poroshenko (Ukrainian president at the time) clashed over the events. Kirill never agreed with the support Bartholomew and his Ecumenical Patriarchate offered to the Ukrainian Orthodox Church and thus essentially permitted the split. This disagreement further reinforced internal strife within the Orthodox Church as Bartholomew of Constantinople is seen as "first among equals" as the oldest in the Eastern Orthodox Church. The European Council on Foreign Relations (specifically, experts Liik, Metodiev, & Popescu, 2019) studied the aftermath of these events and in May 2019 published this quote from Kirill (Gundyaev), the Patriarch of Moscow: "It is impossible for us to separate Kyiv from our country, as this is where our history began. The Russian Orthodox Church preserves the national consciousness of both Russians and Ukrainians." Vladimir Putin echoed him, emphasizing that autocephaly's main objective is to "divide the people of Russia and Ukraine, to sow national and religious divisions."

Liik, Metodiev and Popescu (2019) also reported that communists made good use of the Church, recognizing its influence: during the Second World War, for instance, Josef Stalin ordered Orthodox priests to bless defense lines around the capital. Putin similarly had Orthodox priests bless the missiles destined for Syria as well as Crimea.

After the Second World War the church was believed to be heavily infiltrated by the KGB to act in the state's interest, especially from the 1960s onwards. The Parliamentary Commission created in the early 1990s vindicated this belief.

Whatever Kirill's influence among the non-secular population might be, for his flock, the message was very clear. He is staunchly against an anti-European free secular society which he believes is doomed to fall and, if allowed to influence Russia, will destroy it as well (Karpukhin, 2012).

Again, religion mattered. Religion always matters. Roman Catholic Croatia has been affiliated with the Austro-Hungarian Empire for centuries in the North and with Italy and Venice in the South. In fact, for the better part of 800 years the eastern border of Croatia was the border between Europe (the Austro-Hungarian Empire to which Croatia belonged) and the

Turkish Empire during the Turkish attempts to occupy Europe. The never-ending wars with the "East" reinforced the sense of Catholic identity and affiliation with the "West" among Croats. Hence, in post-Second World War Yugoslavia there was always an uncomfortable union between different religions that harbored centuries of old hatred. The Communists engaged in the active moving of people and combined religious populations, hoping that the mixing bowl would diminish and undo the hatred that existed among various groups of people. However, that policy created the basis of the 1990s conflict.

It is somewhat baffling how the West could have missed the tectonic nature of these events that would be the harbinger of more conflicts to come in light of more than ample recent historic precedents. The West should not have been "surprised" with the invasion of Ukraine. Poland advised Europe for a long time that the invasion was imminent but very few wanted to listen, as described by Mateusz Morawiecki (2022), Prime Minister of Poland.

The interconnections between Balkan history and current Ukrainian conflicts are very complex but also illuminate the current situation as well as events that are likely to emerge in the future. Tim Judah of *The Economist* (political analyst and writer) has created a reputation as an expert in the background and socio-politics of the Balkan conflict. His recent writings very clearly connect the nature of the Serbian aggression in the Balkans with the Putin aggression in Ukraine. Putin often cites Kosovo as an example of how inaction by the East reduces its geopolitical influence. Much like Kosovo, which was Serbia's southern province, Crimea was given to Ukraine by the Soviet Union. While Ukraine was part of the USSR the difference between Crimea's being attached to Ukraine or Russia was irrelevant. An identical situation in Croatia was a "donation" of the city of Neum to Bosnia. This city belonged to Bosnia, while all republics were part of Yugoslavia; that was not relevant, and nobody cared. However, after the split of Croatia, this city split Croatia and made it a noncontiguous country. This realignment led to a flareup of war between Croatia and Bosnia, which was settled relatively quickly. Notice the similarity whereby Crimea, after the split of the USSR, was not only not part of Russia, it was also, even after the invasion by Putin, a noncontiguous territory. A strategic need to have a contiguous territory alone explains the invasion of the Donbas and Luhansk territories. Obviously, its significance and the effect on Russia's access to the Black Sea became astonishingly important after the separation of Ukraine from the USSR.

Talking to Russians and connoisseurs of the culture, one finds out that, while Putin is a polarizing figure, hated by the pro-democracy faction, he is also beloved and supported by vast numbers of people. According to the research published by the Statista Research Department on March 1, 2023, just one month earlier, in February 2023, over 80 percent of Russians approved of Putin's policies and actions. In September 2022, his popularity stood at 77 percent. This was the month when partial mobilization for the war was announced. After Russia invaded Ukraine at the end of February 2022, his approval rating increased.

An example of the "long game" played on religious grounds is the years of consolidation of the Orthodox lines of report and influence in the Serbian Orthodox Church long before the Balkan conflict. The Russian Patriarchate engaged in reinforcing their relationship with the Serb Orthodox Church thus reinforcing the polarizing forces in Yugoslavia.

Thus, there was a long game preparing the people for the carnage that would ensue. The bird's eye view of that conflict can support the view that the Roman Catholic Church in Croatia wanted to flee from the Eastern/Orthodox influence and fulfill its desire to join the EU to which it was religiously and historically more identified. The war more or less forced the hand of the West and, despite an endless delay by the US, was recognized by the international community as an independent country which has since joined the EU and as of January 2023 has adopted the Euro currency. It is highly unlikely that this would have happened without the conflict from the 1990s. The East was yet again wounded and frustrated in its desire to keep territories consolidated since they lost their influence in the western Balkans, including access to nearly the entire northern Adriatic coast; a location that is very important because it is a vast trade and fishing area.

One can't escape the obvious parallels and internal strife that happened in the past. Those strains are also occurring in the present and are likely to occur in the future. Tim Judah of *The Economist* (2023) again wisely draws the parallel of Bosnia's situation, wherein the country was torn apart. The outcome is ongoing bitterness, resentment, and hatred of the "other." In that story, the country (in this case Ukraine) has to deal with the loss of the territories, reinforcement of division and hatred among different intermixed groups of people. Ukrainians in Russian-occupied territories as well as Russians in Ukraine have to manage their day-to-day life dealing with hatred and discrimination. In these territories, the mixtures of peoples led to a "joke" quoted much during the Balkan War. Prior to the war we were all "us" or "we." During the war, if someone approached a front line, they would scream out "don't shoot, I'm one of us," the response was "which us?"

Influence of Economic Interests

When talking to the people in the Balkan areas one finds that they feel that the Ukrainian conflict in many ways is a US vs Russia problem. They are used to looking at the economic motivation of warfare.

A quick glance at the natural resources of Ukraine very rapidly clarifies why NATO and Russia are interested in the country's resources. According to a *Business Today* article (February 2022) Ukraine is globally ranked as:

- Second in gallium extraction.
- Fifth in germanium extraction.
- Sixth in titanium extraction used in surgery and prosthetics and various other applications, most notably airplanes. It is estimated that 20 percent of the total world titanium reserves are in Ukraine.
- Seventh globally in iron extraction ($3.36 billion in iron ore and $2.55 billion in semi-finished iron).
- Eighth globally in manganese extraction.

The country also has no less than three licensed fields and blocks of lithium. This lightweight metal is increasingly of major strategic importance as one of the main components necessary for electric car batteries. Most of the lithium fields are in the Donbas and the Donetsk regions (the Dobra and the Donetsk mines were previously being fought over by Chinese and Australian/European companies).

Ukraine also has three licensed fields and blocks of other rare earth minerals used in smartphones, and seven additional fields and blocks of titanium extraction.

In addition, Ukraine has the second largest reserves of natural gas in Europe, largely unexploited to date (second only to Norway). And the nation is currently dependent on Russia for Asian-sourced gas. Ukraine is a major exporter of edible vegetable oil as well. In addition, 45–55 percent of the global supply of sunflower oil comes from Ukraine; it exports to China ($3.94 billion), Germany $(3.08 billion), Italy (2.57 billion dollars), Poland ($2.75 billion), and to Russia ($4.69 billion).

Finally, Ukraine is a massive source of the world's reserves of corn. It posted $4.7 billion in corn exports. Over 50 percent of the corn exported feeds Africa and the Middle East. Current compromises to get the corn and other grains out of Ukraine are essential as more than 50 million people are on the brink of famine. Taking Ukraine's more than 20 million tons of exported food is of incredible global importance.

As we study the actual economic impact of who influences Ukraine, Putin looks less crazy and more and more like a leader trying to protect his country's strategic and economic interests. Does that justify invading another country? Absolutely not, but it does offer insight into the complicated nature of his character.

Dismissing the Narratives Exacerbates the Problem

Since the invasion of Ukraine, the established narratives about the country have changed rapidly. The West has aggressively dismissed the Russian narrative regarding the threats of neo-Nazi groups in Ukraine. However, in 2018 a Reuters article (Cohen, 2018) very clearly outlined real threats to the population by various right-wing militias in Ukraine and related warnings by a number of Western policy groups and research institutions.

In 2018, Josh Cohen, who wrote for Reuters at the time said, "There's no easy way to eradicate the virulent far-right extremism that has been poisoning Ukrainian politics and public life, but without vigorous and immediate efforts to counteract it, it may soon endanger the state itself" (Cohen, 2018).

That the US government was fully aware of the neo-Nazi problem was clear even then. US Representative Ro Khanna took a clear position against neo-Nazism (Kheel, 2018). He focused on bills that were passed to prohibit the US funds from reaching the Ukrainian troops with neo-Nazi connections, in particular, the notorious Azov Battalion. The article is clear in describing the US support and training of Ukrainian forces in their fight against Russian-backed separatists since 2014. The concern is that portions of the spending bill that included about $620.7 million in aid for Ukraine would reach neo-Nazi-friendly forces.

The Azov Battalion was founded in 2014. Some of the members of the battalion are proud neo-Nazis. In a funny (if it wasn't terrifying) defense of the group, Azov's spokesperson stated to *USA Today* in 2015 (Dorell, 2015) that "only" 10 to 20 percent of recruits are neo-Nazis. Notably, Azov uses Nazi-era symbolism and actively recruits to this day.

According to Miller, a January 28, 2018, demonstration in Kyiv by about 600 members of the "National Militia," an ultranationalist group that promotes the idea that force is necessary to establish order, stormed a city council meeting in the central Ukrainian town of Cherkasy. Their influence led to the passing of a new budget (Miller, 2018).

A recent article in *Foreign Affairs* (Mironova & Sergatskova, 2017) downplayed the risks of the group due to its integration into Ukraine's forces. However, the memory of Slavs is long. The love or hate and the fear of Nazis is very much alive in the memories of people who lived through the horrors of the Second World War, such as young Vladimir Putin through his parents. In other words, it is true that Russian propaganda may have blown the influence of the neo-Nazi movement in Ukraine out of proportion and exaggerated its influence. However, it is equally easy to imagine how a man whose life has been nearly destroyed by Nazis would have an extraordinarily large, trauma-based, response to these reports.

I hope that this chapter helps add breadth and depth to the conflict in Ukraine while highlighting the dangers a further escalation may cause. Failing to consider the additional problems that can emerge if we refuse to consider the full complexities of this war could exacerbate the mounting tensions that already exist.

The current policy of demonizing the opponent, of "throwing labels over the fence," and not communicating, only increases the drift into the "paranoid-schizoid" position.[1]

We are witnessing the consolidation of a totalitarian regime which needs to be understood if we are to prevent escalation. Validation and empathy, used to great effect by therapists, would go a long way in helping us understand the complexities of conflicts around the world. We have to develop a capacity to "walk a mile in their shoes." Empathy for the complex feelings of an average Russian who is supporting Putin is an important step in this process.

Reestablishing communication and understanding the "other" is the only way to de-escalate conflicts.

Another unpopular but inevitable aspect of the conflicts where boundaries, religions, economies, etc. intersect is the need for compromise. The concept of "compromise formation" (Brenner, 2002) is well established in psychoanalytic literature. At this time, no party wants a compromise between what they desire ("id derivative") and what is rationally attainable ("ego and superego workings") which would go a long way in creating peace. It is well established that successful negotiation of best contracts leads to both parties leaving the negotiating table somewhat unhappy but understanding that compromise is necessary. As an example, in the case of Croatia the Croats waited from 1992 until 2022 to make their country a contiguous territory (they had to build a very long bridge to bypass that little city of Neum that belongs to Bosnia). They understood, through the bloodshed of the early days of the war, that compromise was necessary to prevent further bloodshed. We all know that Ukraine and Russia have to sit down and communicate and engage in "compromise formation" hopefully sooner rather than later.

Note

1 Melanie Klein first coined the term "paranoid-schizoid" position in 1946 to describe a primitive mental state wherein an infant can only experience people as all good or all bad. Later she applied this concept to adults.

References

Brenner, C. (2002, July 7). Conflict, compromise formation, and structural theory. *Psychoanalytic Quarterly*, 71(3), 397–417.

Business Today Desk (2022, February 25). Are Ukraine's vast natural resources a real reason behind Russia's invasion. *Business Today*. www.businesstoday.in/latest/world/story/are-ukraines-vast-natural-resources-a-real-reason-behind-russias-invasion-323894-2022-02-25

Cohen, J. (2018, March 19). Commentary: Ukraine's neo-Nazi problem. *Reuters*. www.reuters.com/article/us-cohen-ukraine-commentary/commentary-ukraines-neo-nazi-problem-idUSKBN1GV2TY

Deriglazova, L. (2021, December 9). The Soviet Union's demise as seen by today's Russians. *The Wilson Center*. www.wilsoncenter.org/blog-post/soviet-unions-demise-seen-todays-russians

Dorell, O. (2015, March 10). Volunteer Ukrainian unit includes Nazis. *USA Today*. www.usatoday.com/story/news/world/2015/03/10/ukraine-azov-brigade-nazis-abuses-separatists/24664937/

Hershberg, J. (1995, Issue 5, Spring). Anatomy of a controversy. *The National Security Archive*. George Washington University. https://nsarchive2.gwu.edu/nsa/cuba_mis_cri/moment.htm

Interfax-Ukraine (2021, March 12). Zelensky: Forget that Ukraine to forget about Crimea. *Kyiv Post*. https://archive.kyivpost.com/ukraine-politics/zelensky-forget-that-ukraine-to-forget-about-crimea.html

Judah, T. (2023, January 11). Reconstructing Ukraine. *The New York Review of Books*. www.nybooks.com/online/2023/01/11/reconstructing-ukraine/

Karpukhin, S. (2012, February 9). Russian orthodox patriarch Kirill calls Putin era a "miracle of God." Reuters. www.reuters.com/article/idUK408811938120120209

Kheel, R. (2018, March 27). Congress bans arms to Ukraine militia linked to neo-Nazis. *Website of Congressman Ro Khanna*. https://khanna.house.gov/media/in-the-news/congress-bans-arms-ukraine-militia-linked-neo-nazis

Liik, K., Metodiev, M., & Popescu, N. (2019, May 30). Defender of the faith. How Ukraine's Orthodox split threatens Russia. *European Council of Foreign Relations*. https://ecfr.eu/publication/defender_of_the_faith_how_ukraines_orthodox_split_threatens_russia/

Mamo, C. (2021, March 3). Explainer: The split in the Ukraine's Orthodox Church. *Emerging Europe*. https://emerging-europe.com/news/the-explainer-the-split-in-ukraines-orthodox-church/

Miller, C. (2018, January 31). In Ukraine, ultranationalist militia strikes fear in some quarters. *RadioFreeEurope/RadioLiberty*. www.rferl.org/a/ukraine-azov-right-wing-militia-to-patrol-kyiv/29008036.html

Mironova, V., & Sergatskova, E. (2017, August 1). How Ukraine retained its militias. *Foreign Affairs*. www.foreignaffairs.com/articles/ukraine/2017-08-01/how-ukraine-reined-its-militias

Morawiecki, M. (2022, February 25). Polish PM: Europe must abandon all illusions about Russia. *FT.com*. https://www.ft.com/content/315a342d-d646-4061-ab4a-d2455b6a7221

Saikali, E. (2023, January 9). Patriarch Kirill: The politically influential head of the Russian Orthodox Church. *France24.com*. www.france24.com/en/europe/20230109-patriarch-kirill-the-politically-influential-head-of-the-russian-orthodox-church

Statista.com (2023, March). Do you approve of the activities of Vladimir Putin as the president (prime minister) of Russia? *Stastia.com*. www.statista.com/statistics/896181/putin-approval-rating-russia/

Watson Institute International and Public Affairs. (2021, August). Human and budgetary costs to date of the US war in Afghanistan, 2001–2021. Brown University. https://watson.brown.edu/costsofwar/figures/2021/human-and-budgetary-costs-date-us-war-afghanistan-2001-2022

PART 3

Investigating Vladimir Putin's Personality

How Trauma Affected His Development

Chapter 4

Zeitenwende

Vladimir Putin's Effort to Reestablish the Russian/Post Soviet Empire

Peter W. Petschauer

Introduction

When German Chancellor Olaf Scholz on February 27, 2022, spoke of coming change, he meant that Russia's attack on Ukraine on February 24, 2022, was a battle for the ages. Even if the statement came in the heat of the moment—the attack on a neighboring independent European country—the German leader reflected the sense of people across Europe, namely that the assumption of the viability of European peace had been upended ... the peace that had lasted, with some short and less significant interruptions, on the continent for more than seven decades, since 1945, had come to an end.

Why did we assume that this peace could last for another few generations? After all, we had come this far without a major war. Even those "in the know" underestimated the eagerness of someone on their periphery who would sooner or later launch an attack to realign what seemed like established borders. Most Westerners, even many Ukrainians, underestimated Vladimir Vladimirovich Putin's eagerness to violate the borders of an independent European nation and attempt to absorb it into his state; this is what he meant when he called Ukraine a brother state.

Elaboration

In some ways Vladimir Vladimirovich Putin's upbringing was typical in Soviet Russia: a humble but intact family background in the authoritarian setting of Leningrad, plus a history of youthful troublemaking. However, the roots of his later advance into Ukraine may be linked to an overall feeling of being "surrounded" and in Russia's complicated position as a crumbling empire threatened by the "outside world." Such context may help explain Putin's urge to reestablish an idealized past (Short, 2022).

That was not all; Putin could not escape Russia's recent history. Leningrad had suffered terribly under the German encirclement, and WWII affected his father and mother. The senior Putin was seriously wounded at the front and severely traumatized as a result, and sometimes he reflected both on the glories and miseries of the Great Patriotic War, as Russians called the conflict. Putin's mother nearly died of starvation, like her infant son, but was saved at the last moment when she was already selected to be carted off, considered dead. She coped with her trauma through care for her son. As normal as Putin's childhood was in some ways, he was born into a transgenerationally traumatized family in October 1952 (Müller, 2002).[1]

Although an experience sometimes ignored, he would have internalized views of the massive destruction of his city. He absorbed stories of Nazi aggression and the surrounding of his city that overlapped with being restrained as an infant and being overly protected in an authoritarian household. A rebellious rowdy, a *gopnik*, he realized early enough that this style of life would lead to jail (Elovitz, 2022, pp. 320–325).[2]

How does one escape such environments? As a group, Russians responded in at least three ways. One was to attempt to forget past traumas with lots of alcohol and violence against others, especially in the immediate household; another was to build up a sense of being powerful, superior, chosen even; still another was to reach outward to others, as a country, to other nations; often in war.

Let me tackle the first question by saying that Putin did not take the path of alcohol, but violence, including the aggressiveness toward the boys in his neighborhood and later toward his first wife, which probably stems from his sense of being "less than." But he has in the past also seen himself as an archer, a hunter, a jet pilot, a motorcycle rider. (Such images were widely shared in Russian and Western news outlets.)

The second of these options is more difficult to pinpoint. When did Putin notice that he had been given the same name as Vladimir the Great of Kyiv? What reflections accompanied this recognition? We don't know fully, but he may well have compensated for his small stature with his aggressiveness as a teen and his discovery of a major figure in the past. Many of us in the older generation, this author included, at some point associated our name with a figure in the past. Mine was St. Peter. Putin may have learned about the saint and conqueror and overcome some of the negative feelings that he tried to overcome by aligning himself with this historical figure and, more recently, with Peter the Great for different reasons. Of his historical heroes, both Vladimir and Peter rose to prominence in the eyes of their contemporaries and later observers as reformers and conquerors, with historians usually overlooking their unspeakable brutality. Vladimir was a perfect model for Putin. Vladimir the Great's sculpture outside the Kremlin says it all. He turned to Greek Orthodoxy and this shores up Putin's stance on several issues, including behavior unbefitting a Christian, like excessive alcohol use and homosexuality (Ihanus, 2022, pp. 300–305). Then there is Peter I. Only specialists know about his abused childhood, his miserable treatment of his aides, and his torturing and murdering his son.

This part of Putin's life points to two very important aspects of it: His own unique understanding of Russian history and, interwoven with it, his own life story; he is situated in the middle of that vast state's past and present.

When we view Putin, we see almost as many perspectives as we hear or read from his observers. In the 1980s he was perceived as a forward-looking Russian politician, who, in spite of his stint in the military and KGB, was eager to work with Western Europe and the US. For example, he met with French President Emmanuel Macron and spoke in Germany's parliament, in perfectly good German. Even before then, during his time in St. Petersburg as an economic developer, he seemed open to cooperation with Western business contacts (interview with a former negotiator, April 17, 2022).

In addition to this, one cannot fully understand Putin's approach to life without knowing that Muscovy's rulers expanded their territories through marriage, purchase, murder, and war. They also adopted the attitudes and ways of outsiders, especially Westerners. Ivan III, also known as Ivan the Great and one of the most astute of the Muscovite rulers, sought contact with the last of the Byzantine family and, after the death of his first wife, married Sophia Paleologos, a niece of the last Byzantine ruler. Ivan was thus able to take on the mantle of successor not only to that empire, but also that of Rome. Moscow now thought of itself as the Third Rome, and Ivan called himself, *czar*, Russian for Caesar.

Most likely persuaded by his wife, who had been brought up in Rome, he hired Italian specialists in everything from goldsmiths to architects; some of their accomplishments are still visible in the Kremlin today (Fennell, 1961). That Ivan III had additional contacts with the West emerges from the account of the mission of Baron Sigismund von Herberstein to Moscow (one of the earliest German versions is *Moscovia der Hauptstat in Reissen* [Russia], 1557).

The lure of the West continued with Ivan the Terrible, Ivan III's grandson. As would happen often later, Ivan could not understand Elizabeth I of England's reluctance to deal with him (Bertolet, 2011). Ivan's attempts were interrupted, soon after his death, by massive invasions of Muscovy from all sides; Polish troops celebrated in the Kremlin at the outset of the 17th century.

Fast forward to the end of that century and Peter the Great's exploratory trip to Western Europe. He was persuaded by his foreign advisers that he needed to learn about Europe, adopt European ways, and establish contacts with Western monarchs (an exhibit of aspects of the trip is available at Kunstkamera.ru/en/museum/kunst_his/5/5_1). He was also persuaded that Russia needed a warm water port. When his attempt to capture the city of Azov failed, he turned his attention to the north, entering the Swedish territory along the Baltic and encountering its brilliant king, Charles X. In response the Swedish king marched as far south as today's Ukraine, but at

Poltava, Peter pushed him back and incorporated areas along the Baltic and Eastern Ukraine. Subsequently he called himself *czar* and emperor.

With Peter, the Russian elite became Western and rulers like Anna, Elizabeth, and Catherine II reinforced this trend. In the second half of the century, the seemingly insignificant German princess named Sophie usurped the Imperial throne, renamed herself, and heavily leaned toward Europe in her attempts to reform everything from government to nobility. She had visited most courts in the then Germanies as a teen and very much fit in with their conversations, styles, and aspirations; in addition, her father was a Prussian field marshal for Fredrick II. No wonder Catherine supported her lovers and generals as they acquired parts of Poland and also took in most of today's Ukraine and thus access to the Black Sea in the 1770s, 1780s, and 1791 from the Ottoman Empire. Western and enlightened, yet a conqueror.

Upon Catherine's grandson, Alexander I, a totally westernized man and reformer, fell the job of restraining Napoleon's attack in 1812. By playing a major role in defeating the French emperor, Russia entered European affairs further and also gained Finland. If there was a point at which the myth of encirclement gained adherents in the upper layers of Russian society, it was when his internationally staffed army of Napoleon encamped in Moscow. The story of the ordinary peasant fortunate enough to avoid this vast force does not appear in the annals of Russian history, for they had other worries.

It is difficult to say if the fear of being trapped was introduced or reinforced in the population as a whole by Imperial Germany's advance into Russia in 1918. But the three-pronged Hitlerite attack of 1941 may have accomplished this perception. German troops stood a few kilometers before Moscow, encircled Leningrad, and pressed as far east as the Caucasus. The Soviet response was based not just on the invasion itself, but also on the fierce brutality against practically every ethnic group and person in a leadership role in the country. Stalin's equally brutal counterattack gave him Eastern Europe and reinforced the hold on Central Asia.

We may look for this sense of being trapped inside, whether simply situated in the upper layers of Russian society or throughout all parts of it, not just because of outside invasions. It is also because of restraining and holding abuses in childhood. Until recently, most Russian children lived and learned in strict households and schools (about current practices in Russian society, see https://taz.de/Erziehung-in-Russland/!5862350/). The principal family in Grossman's *Stalingrad* (Grossman, 2019) is the exception, not the rule.

The first post-war contact between Russia and the West was initiated in the early 1960s. The rapprochement reverberated with Westerners and tours visiting the Soviet Union, and business, political, and academic contacts followed. In the early 1970s, my university, Appalachian State University, first began internal conversations about student and faculty exchanges in the Soviet Union. We established a contact with the North Ossetian State University in Vladikavkaz in the early 1980s.[3]

The long path both of Russia into Europe and vice versa now seemed complete (Malia, 1996). Contrary to reprimands today about these contacts and connections, the hope on both sides was to link Russia and the West. Especially after the horrific experience of World War II, it seemed the best way to move forward, both potentially to ease the burdens of the people in Eastern Europe and assist Russia in its valiant attempts to recover. Full expression of this hope emerged with Mikhail Gorbachev's *glasnost* (openness) and *perestroika* (restructuring).

Gorbachev believed that he could undertake reforms because the West and Russians would support him. The enthusiasm was palatable. My colleague who taught at Ulan Bator during Gorbachev's reforms recalled his own and his colleagues' enthusiastic support (interview with Professor Anatoly Isaenko, 2011).

But "reality intervened." Gorbachev wanted to reform the system peacefully, but the system could not take the strain (Taubman, 2017). The various bureaucracies, including the secret police, the military, and the communist party apparatus were too entrenched, and undermined the effort. Putin grew up during this shake-up. Successful and comfortable in the system, he was one of those troubled by *perestroika* and *glasnost*. Gorbachev lost control when the "nations" (ethnic-centered states within the Soviet Union) took this new openness as their cue to demand their separation from the Union. When the Soviet Union fell apart in 1991, the leaders of the West heeded the call for help to build democracies in Eastern Europe and protect themselves from Russia; one can interpret the agreements of the 1990s between Russia and NATO as efforts to gain greater influence eastward. It should not be a surprise that Putin never forgave Gorbachev for the outcome of his reform efforts, namely the collapse of the Soviet Union and, with time, to see NATO's move eastward as a threat.

The question remains: Why did Vladimir Putin decide to invade Ukraine when he did? And how could one misinterpret the meaning of the thousands of troops, tanks, trucks, and planes at the border of Ukraine? Part of the answer is that it is easy to ignore unwanted realities, like climate change and the background of autocratic decision-makers. In Putin's case, most opinion-makers, reflected in the media, were unaware of his upbringing, his aggressiveness as a teen, his harsh treatment of his first wife in Dresden, his acute awareness of Russian history, and Imperial and Soviet entanglements with the outside world.

European leaders thought that he was bluffing in trying to rid Ukraine of Volodymyr Zelensky, and to bring Ukraine back into Russia's sphere of influence (Vincent, 2022). On the other hand, the American intelligence services had already warned in mid-2021 of a potential Russian invasion of

Ukraine. This awareness is significantly different from earlier American leaders who failed to heed warnings about Adolf Hitler's intentions to wage war on the rest of Europe. American Chargé d'Affaires Alexander Kirk smiled in the embassy in Berlin in the summer of 1939 when Donald Heath informed him "that he had received intelligence indicating that 'Nazi military aggression would shortly occur'" (Donner, 2021). Heath and members of the resistance had been warning the US leadership for some time about the situation. The leadership chose not to listen. Why attack?

While the public as a whole was hoping against hope, or ignorant of the situation altogether, during the middle of 2021 Putin reflected on what to do (Short, 2022, p. 630ff, especially note 108). As a historian with psychological training, I must investigate what he said at the time and be aware of his background as a survivor of over-protective swaddling, an authoritarian household, and stories of Leningrad's encirclement during World War II. He grew into a ruffian, a KGB agent, a wife beater, and yet also an astute reader of Russian history, with an intense sense of loss about the collapse of the Soviet Union and with it the loss of Ukraine to Russia. He was also thinking of retiring, and with that about his legacy (Short, 2022, pp. 650–652); by the summer of 2021, his desire to rid Ukraine of Volodymyr Zelensky and to reintegrate Ukraine into the Russian fold had become his highest priorities.

His excuse for invading Ukraine holds true in one sense and not in another. One may argue that Kyiv was the original capital of Russia, as I did as part of Russian history courses (based especially on Riasanovsky, 1999) and Muscovy emerged from it later. If anything, Kyiv should be the capital of Russia. But the reality is that, with the death of Ivan the Terrible, the last viable ruler of the Rurik dynasty, the link with Kyiv broke and Ukraine had to be reunited with Russia by conquest, that of Peter the Great and Catherine the Great. In other words, the tale of Ukraine as always having been Russian is not sustainable. Rather, Kyiv was an independent state during the Middle Ages and then conquered by Russia in the 18th century.

Another reality is that by the end of the first decade of the 21st century, NATO had become a shadow of itself; but it began to regain its footing after the annexation of Crimea in March of 2014 (Frye, 2021, p. 166) and with it inspired imagined or real fears in Putin of being surrounded.

When Zelensky made clear his intention that Ukraine did not want to return to the Russian orbit, force remained as the only option. Based on the example of Chechnya and Crimea, Putin calculated that the West would not interfere in a move on Ukraine. He also thought that any Western blockades would not hurt Russia's economy further and that Ukraine's military, even with Western support, could not withstand the massive force he had already begun to assemble. He asked for and received the support of his most immediate cadres and was assured in addition to the support of the Duma, the legislative chamber of Russia's parliament, that he had already begun to eliminate most opposition. He obtained China's quietude.

But the timing needed to be perfect. Putin wanted a short war, one like the Crimea offensive in March 2014, and because tanks and other heavy equipment do best on frozen ground, he chose the end of February. He thought that Kyiv would fall immediately and Zelensky leave the country. Like Putin, most Western observers agreed that the Ukrainians would be routed quickly. One never knows the outcome of a war once it has started.

Putin definitely did not anticipate that Ukraine and the West would not cave immediately. He found himself, like many leaders in the past, bent on a short war, and, like many others before him, instead facing a long-drawn-out conflict and in some cases a regime change. A long conflict meant that another Russian reality came into play. Its warfare had taken on several horrific dimensions even before Putin rose to power; earlier Russian leaders demonstrated a penchant for uniquely violent approaches to civilians and war. For example, Nicholas I destroyed towns in the Caucasus with long-range cannons. Stalin starved millions of Ukrainians in the mid-1930s and sent at least 28 million Russians to Siberia. Learning from the Germans, British, and Americans, he ordered European cities bombed into oblivion. In that tradition, Putin, aside from seeing Nazis "everywhere" in a time-collapsed fashion, has civilians starved and prisoners beaten and killed, and cities bombed into near oblivion.

Conclusion

So, why did Putin do it? Why did he order the attack? Why invade a sovereign country? The best answer is: That he had become an authoritarian ruler and he could. Rare is the authoritarian who does not start a war! But there is also the uniqueness of his early years, the stories of Leningrad's misery, the Nazi aggression, the lost glory of the Soviet Union, and NATO's threatening eastward move. He thought he could win quickly and do so with impunity and without accountability.

He is not the first autocrat to miscalculate his chances of success, even recalling Russian history selectively. He was not thinking of Nicholas II nor of Gorbachev, except dismissively. He compensated for his small stature by associating himself with his namesake Vladimir and the other great, Peter I, sees "Nazis" everywhere, and is certain of Western corruption, in large part because of what he perceives as the failures of democracies. His successes in Chechnya, Syria, Crimea and, to an extent, the Donbas inspired him to launch a "short war" against Ukraine. Those who believe that he responded to NATO's expansion are missing the contacts between it and Russia after the collapse of the Soviet Union and Putin's early efforts to cooperate with the West, a major aspect of Russia's history since the late Middle Ages. But I rather also highlight his stated disappointment with the collapse of the

Soviet Union and his fears about NATO's hidden aims and Ukraine's turning even more fully to the West. He definitely wanted to retain it in Russia's fold.

I am grateful to Dr. Paul Elovitz, Nicole D'Andria, Dr. Angela Moré, and Dr. Brigitte Demeure for their assistance in preparing this chapter.

Notes

1 Unfortunately, this article is no longer available.
2 My first view as a child of the remaining devastation of Cologne in 1951 sits deeply in my consciousness and shapes my view of war to this day.
3 I was delighted to be in Moscow and Leningrad in the mid-1960s.

References

Bertolet, A.R. (2011). The Tsar and the Queen: "You speak a language that i understand not." In Beem, C. (ed.) *The Foreign Relations of Elizabeth I. Queenship and Power*. Palgrave Macmillan. https://doi.org/10.1057/9780230118553_5

Donner, Rebecca. (2021). *All the frequent troubles of our days. The true story of the American woman at the heart of the German resistance to Hitler*. Little, Brown and Company, p. 295.

Elovitz, Paul. (2022). Mother Russia's savior, traumatic reenactment, and the atrocities of war. *Clio's Psyche*, 28, 3 [Spring], pp. 320–325.

Fennell, John. L.I. (1961). *Ivan the Great of Moscow*. Macmillan.

Frye, Timothy. (2021). *Weak strongman. The limits of power in Putin's Russia*. Princeton University Press, p. 166.

Grossman, Vasily. (2019). *Stalingrad* (Robert and Elizabeth Chandler, trans.). NYRB Classics.

Ihanus, Juhani. (2022). Putin and Ukraine. Putin, Ukraine and fratricide. *Clio's Psyche*, 28, 3 [Spring], pp. 300–305.

Malia, Martin. (1996). *Russia under Western Eyes: From the Bronze Horseman to the Lenin Mausoleum*. Belknap Press.

Moscovia der Hauptstat in Reissen [Russia] (1557). Vienna.

Müller, Julius (2002, March 13). Kind traumatisierter Eltern: Woher kommt Putins Brutalität? *Ausburger Allgemeine*.

Riasanovsky, Nicholas (1999). *A history of Russia*. Oxford University Press.

Taubman, William (2017). *Gorbachev. His Life and times*. W.W. Norton.

Taz. (2022, May 7) Erziehung in Russland. Gewalt von Kinderbeinen an. *Taz*. https://taz.de/Erziehung-in-Russland/!5862350/

Vincent, Elise. (2022, March 6). Interview with General Thierry Burkhard, the French Chief of Staff. *Le Monde*.

Chapter 5

Invasion of Ukraine

Observations on Leader–Follower Relationships[1]

Vamik Volkan and Jana D. Javakhishvili

On February 24, 2022, Russia launched an invasion of Ukraine, and the world began witnessing horrifying events unfold and brutality take place against civilians and innocents. We are reminded of sociologist and former US Undersecretary of Defense for Policy Fred Charles Ikle's (1971) statement that there has never been a period in history without men acquiring positions of power who were willing to die, and to see others die, for causes that they themselves invented and which were espoused by only a few of their henchmen. In several countries the political process is such that leaders can come to the top and consider it a virtue, or perhaps part of their "revolutionary" creed, to live dangerously. "Vivere pericolosamente" ("to live dangerously") was one of Benito Mussolini's favorite slogans (p. 127).

Political Leaders' Personalities

Minimizing the role of a leader's personality in scholarly essays on historical or political processes most likely has been related to the dominant role of the so-called "rational actor" models in international and domestic affairs. These models have continued to influence politicians and scholars since the middle of the last century (von Rochau, 1853). They supported the assumption that a political leader's decision-making is logical and unaffected by psychological factors, especially within countries where democratic principles prevail.

One example comes from a dialogue between David Ben-Gurion, who is considered the "father" of the state of Israel, and the Israeli historian Yehoshua Arieli. Ben-Gurion asked Arieli whether the personalities of political leaders were important in history. Arieli responded by saying that the answer depended on many factors such as the times, historical conditions, the social and political system, and, of course, the individual's stature in government; his answer was a qualified "yes." Ben-Gurion, however, interrupted Arieli by stating that history is made by the nation, not by leaders (Malkin & Zhahor, 1992). In writing this chapter we are taking Arieli's side in his encounter with the Israeli leader.

Examining and reaching conclusions from a distance about the personality organization of a political leader such as Putin raises serious questions. Early psychoanalytic writings on the lives of famous artists and historical figures primarily focused on interpreting the symbols they employed, such as those used by artists in their works, but these interpretations did not attempt to identify what accounted for the directions of such creativity.

Later, when psychoanalysis became better established, psychoanalytic writers began considering more than one causal factor when investigating an individual's artistic work, political ideology, or drastic constructive or destructive actions.

Knowledge gained through studying child development led to a focus on the actual life history of the biographical subject. Childhood traumas began to attract considerable attention. The biographer sought to know why this or that ego function was overdeveloped or underdeveloped, how the ego mediated between different mental demands, and what kinds of defensive or sublimated adaptations to one's living conditions were made.

Erik Erikson (1958) changed the character of psychobiography and suggested that the biographer should focus on the adolescent years, a time when a person's horizons expand beyond family and neighbors to a wider social sphere. Later, historical situations in the life of a young adult, as well as mid-life crises, were considered by psychoanalytic biographers in general (Bergmann, 1973).

In the late 1980s, a group of psychoanalysts and psychiatrists formed a committee to study the psychodynamics of international relations. The group met twice a year for five years and engaged in a dialogue both among themselves and with many others in various disciplines, including historians, political scientists, and former diplomats. These participants studied personality organizations of different political leaders, for example, American presidents Woodrow Wilson, Richard Nixon, John Kennedy, and also leaders from other locations, including world leaders Anwar Sadat, Saddam Hussein, and Slobodan Milošević. They concluded:

Leaders make decisions that cannot always be explained by conventional, rational approaches to domestic and international decision-making. When the individual psychology of a decision-maker is "agitated" by external factors in the political environment, emotions and psychodynamic responses, whether acknowledged or not, can drastically influence decisions. On the other hand, decision-makers who have an "agitated" internal world may make decisions that attempt to affect or change the external world in order to find a "solution" for the leader's unconscious needs or wishes (Volkan et al., 1998, pp. 171–172).

One of the authors of this chapter, Vamık Volkan, working with others and also alone, has written psycho-biographies of the founder of the Turkish Republic Kemal Atatürk (Volkan & Itzkowitz, 1984); Richard Nixon (Volkan et al., 1997); Abdullah Öcalan, the founder of

Kurdish Workers' Party (PKK) who started a campaign of terror in Turkey in 1984 (Volkan, 1997); and Slobodan Milošević, the Serbian leader after the collapse of the former Yugoslavia (Volkan, 2013). Research for all these books involved interviewing individuals who knew the leaders or who knew the leaders' families. These accounts from actual observations provided useful data.

Volkan and his co-authors used a developmental approach in writing a psychobiography. First, they examined information from the subject's infancy and early childhood, including the dyadic relationship between child and mother, the construction of the subject's unconscious fantasies, and the mother's (and other caretakers') unconscious fantasies about the child, all of which influence the subject's formation of a sense of self. They also investigated the subject's early traumas, developmental arrests, early symptom formation and adaptation to the environment, growth-inducing experiences, the nature of the subject's oedipal struggles and the crystallization of the personality organization during the adolescent passage.

Second, they focused on the adult subject's internal responses to external events, attempts to change the environment to fit internal demands, activities in the service of maintaining self-esteem, affective expressions or affect control, sexual adaptation, choosing of mates, and responses to parenthood. Finally, an inquiry was made into transformations of identity, regressions, and subsequent progressions in the reconsolidation of identity, mid-life issues, and reactions to aging and the approach to death. Thus, the subject's entire life is looked at developmentally through a psychoanalytic lens.

Obviously, the degree of success that can be achieved in writing a psychoanalytic psychobiography through the application of this developmental approach depends on the availability of information about the subject. Furthermore, especially when writing the psychobiography of a political figure, it will be imperative for the biographer to have sufficient information about the political culture and conditions surrounding the subject and the political figure's ethnic, national, religious, or ideological large-group identity.

Putin's Background

The authors of this chapter never met Putin or any individual who had interactions with this political leader of Russia. We lack the information needed for an in-depth analysis of his personality organization.

Putin was born in 1952, when his mother was 41 years old, and his father was also in his 40s. His parents had lost two children before Putin's birth. One, Albert, died in infancy before World War II, while the other one, Viktor, died during the blockade of Leningrad (the Soviet-era name for St. Petersburg) (Putin et al., 2000). From September 1941 to January 1944 Leningrad was blockaded by the Nazis.

In January 2012, Putin briefly shared the story of his family's World War II experience on the war's anniversary while attending the annual wreath-laying at Piskaryovskoye Cemetery in St. Petersburg, a place where 470,000 civilians and soldiers were buried in mass graves (https://ria.ru/20150430/1061653827.html). He stated:

> My parents told me that children were taken from their families in 1941, and my mother had a child (three-year-old Victor) taken from her—with the goal of saving him … They said he had died, but they never said where he was buried.
>
> (Barry, 2012, p. 9)

Putin was his parents' third son, born about ten years after Victor's death. He is the only child to survive. It is known that Putin visited Piskaryovskoye Cemetery most years to commemorate the horrible German blockade. According to experts' estimations, during this blockade, 600,000 to 1.5 million Russians died of starvation (Reid, 2011). We also know that in 2000, 12 years after Putin became the president of Russia, an organization called "We Remember Them All by Name" attempted to find where Victor had been buried in 1942. In 2014 this organization concluded that Victor was in one of the mass graves. We have no evidence indicating that Putin ordered this organization to find his dead brother's grave and possible remains. Putin (2015) himself wrote that people he did not know "on their own initiative" found documents concerning his brother.

In the book, *First Person: An Astonishingly Frank Self-Portrait by Russia's President* (Putin et al., 2000), Putin speaks more about his family's experience during the Nazi blockade of Leningrad. He was told that once his starving mother had lost consciousness and was laid out by some government officials alongside those who had died of hunger. She was going to be transported for burial along with the corpses. Luckily, she moaned and thus was not buried together with the dead.

Putin's father was a veteran soldier who had fought and suffered a leg wound caused by a direct grenade pelting by German soldiers. He lived the rest of his life with shrapnel in his leg. In 2015 Putin revealed that the person who witnessed his mother's body next to the corpses and noted that she was still breathing was his father. He had just come from the hospital where he had received treatment. After he realized that his wife was alive, government officials still suggested that he give them permission to transport her body, believing that she would die anyway before they reached the mass grave. Putin wrote how his father attacked the government officials with his crutches and forced them to return his wife to the family apartment. It was Putin's father who saved Putin's mother's life. She lived until 1999, after losing her husband in 1998. There were other losses in Putin's family during World War II. His mother's mother was shot by Germans when they occupied

Tver City, and it is reported that five of his uncles from his father's side and two (some say five) of his mother's other relatives also died during the war.

Putin (2015) wrote that his father did not want to talk about the family's war experiences. But as Putin was growing up, he would listen when his father and mother had conversations about what had happened to the family during the war. He recalled that sometimes his parents directly turned to him and included him in these conversations. He also noted that his parents did not hate the enemy and added that he, frankly, could not understand this attitude.

Putin (2015) describes his mother as a "gentle person" In the book, where he is referred to as the "First Person" he writes about how his father had beaten him with a belt when he was either of preschool age or as a student in a primary school. The reason for his punishment was that little Putin had gone out with his friends on a train away from his home. In the book, Putin states that after this incident he lost his desire to travel without his parents' permission. However, we do not know if Putin as a child faced repeated physical trauma or if this beating by his father was an isolated incident. At the time, this kind of punishment might have been considered a normal and acceptable method of childrearing.

We are aware of Polish journalist Krystyna Kurczap-Redlich's 2016 book about Putin and her claiming a different background for the Russian president. According to this author, well-known in Poland, Vovka (Putin) was born in 1950 after his mother had a love affair with a married man. The mother left the baby with her parents, who were living near the Ural Mountains. She met a man from Georgia, married him and moved to Georgia. Initially Vovka (Putin) was brought to Georgia, but because the stepfather was a violent person, the child's mother sent her son back to her maternal grandparents. In turn the grandparents gave the boy to a family who were relatives living in St. Petersburg who had lost two children. Krystyna Kurczap-Redlich claims that Putin's biological mother, in her 90s, still lives in the Republic of Georgia and that Kurczap-Redlich had visited her.

One of us, Jana Javakhishvili, read the Polish journalist's book and watched her recent video presentation. We also consulted with colleagues in Russia and concluded that at the present time we have no clear evidence to support Kurczap-Redlich's claims.

Invasion of Ukraine: Observations, Rescue Fantasies, and Replacement Child Phenomenon

In psychoanalytic clinical practice we observe "rescue fantasies" in analysands whose families had traumatic losses. During their childhood or while going through adolescence, such analysands had mothers (or other caretakers with mothering functions) who were depressed, who were missing, or who were not able to provide adequate mothering. At the same time, these children or youngsters could not "reach up" to a father or father figure to find a nurturing object. Their unconscious fantasy of saving the mother from her depression and bringing her back to function as a mother is to induce an illusion of having a good mothering experience. The "mental content" of a rescue fantasy may lead to maladaptive or adaptive compromise formations during the individual's adulthood (Abend, 2008; Arlow, 1969; Beres, 1962; Inderbitzin & Levy, 1990; Volkan, 1981, 2010).

A child's developing rescue fantasies receive support if this child is perceived by his or her mother (or mothering persons) as a "replacement child." A mother has an internalized image of her child who has died. She deposits, or transgenerationally transports (Kestenberg & Brenner, 1996; Kogan, 1995; Laub & Auerhahn, 1993), this image into the developing self-representation of her next-born child, usually born after the first child's death. The second child, the "replacement child" (Ainslie & Solyom, 1986; Cain & Cain, 1964; Green & Solnit, 1964; Legg & Sherick, 1976; Poznanski, 1972; Volkan & Ast, 1997), has no actual experience with the dead sibling or with his or her image. The mother, who has an image of the dead child, treats the second one as the reservoir where the dead child can be kept "alive." Accordingly, the mother gives, mostly unconsciously, the second child certain ego tasks to protect and maintain what is deposited in this child.

Replacement children develop personal ego functions to deal with what has been pushed into them. For example, replacement children will be preoccupied with the task of integrating the deposited image with the rest of their self-representation. These children may or may not succeed in doing so. If the task is successful, the replacement child will not exhibit psychopathology. If this task is not successful, replacement children may develop an unintegrated self-representation.

In the replacement child phenomenon, there may also be some depositing of the depositor's injured self-image into the child's self. Some adults may actively, but mostly unconsciously, push their own traumatized self-images and traumatized object-images, whether they are connected with a concrete loss or not, into developing self-representations of their children. The actual memories of the trauma belong to adults; children have no experience with the trauma. Clearly, memories belonging to one person cannot be transmitted to another person, but an adult can deposit traumatized self-images and object-images as well as others, such as realistic or imagined object-images that are formed in the depositor's mind as a response to trauma, into a child's self-representation. This process may or may not be a source of pathology depending on how the child handles what had been "deposited" by the traumatized adult into his or her internal world.

George Pollock (1975) gathered data on artists, scientists, and political leaders and pundits concerning their childhood experiences with death. He found that loss does not necessarily account for the creative act or the creative product, but the creative act may be given direction by childhood loss. Similar findings appeared in other psychoanalytic studies (see Hamilton, 1969, 1979; Wolfenstein, 1973; Plank & Plank, 1978). Stanley Olinick (1980) wondered what makes a person pursue a career as a psychoanalyst. He wrote about how unconscious rescue fantasies play a key role in directing individuals to become psychoanalysts. Volkan (2010) concluded, as George Pollock had done, that rescue fantasies have pushed many individuals to search out leadership roles, including political ones.

What we need to keep in mind is that some leaders influenced by such a fantasy become reparative leaders who increase the self-esteem of their ethnic, national, religious, or ideological large groups without hurting and destroying or oppressing another large group. Kemal Atatürk was a replacement child; his mother lost three children and her husband when her son was a child. Volkan and Itzkowitz (1984) describe in detail how the Turkish leader verbalized his rescue fantasy in words and deeds. He became the "savior" of the Turks after the collapse of the Ottoman Empire.

Other political leaders become destructive leaders, even criminal bullies like Putin, who deliberately initiate inhumane actions and oppress and injure innocent people in order to raise primarily their own and their followers' narcissism (Volkan, 2004, 2020).

Putin's Adult Life

It is beyond the aim of this chapter to give detailed information about Vladimir Putin's adult life. Briefly, after studying law at Leningrad State University he worked as a KGB foreign intelligence officer for 16 years. In 1983, Putin married Lyudmila Shkrebneva, a stewardess for Aeroflot. From this marriage Putin has two daughters and two grandsons. Putin and his wife divorced in 2014, allegedly because of Putin's extramarital relationship with former Olympic gymnast Alina Kabaeva, with whom he reportedly fathered four children. It is also alleged that Putin has another "secret" love child, a daughter. Without having detailed information about Putin's love life and his many children, we have no idea if these issues are unconsciously connected to his fantasies about his dead brothers; we will not focus on these issues in this chapter.

In 1996 Putin joined the administration of Boris Yeltsin, who was appointed as prime minister in August 1999. After Yeltsin's resignation, Putin became acting president, and four months later was elected president and served two terms. In the period from 2008 to 2012 he served as head of the Government of the Russian Federation while Dmitri Medvedev, strongly supported by Putin, became president for one term. In 2012 Putin was reelected president for the third time. And as we are writing this paper, he is still the president of his country, after his election to this position for the fourth time, in 2018. In 2020 changes were implemented in the

Russian constitution allowing him to run in the elections in 2024 as well (Belton, 2020; Myers, 2015; Roxburgh, 2013).

After World War II and then the collapse of the Soviet Union, the newly independent former Soviet states started to move toward democracy. This path brought many challenges—undigested totalitarian trauma and totalitarian inertia (Javakhishvili, 2014, 2018; Schmidt-Löw-Beer, Atria & Davar, 2015), a longtime tradition of corruption, socio-economic turmoil, inter-ethnic political tensions—many designed in the Soviet period based on the "Divide et Impera" (Divide and rule) principle inherited by Russia, which led to the wave of military conflicts, catalyzed by institutionalized identity divisions. Since 2000, under the rule of Vladimir Putin, democracy in Russia has gradually deteriorated.

Rescue Fantasies

Putin, as a replacement child, had an unconscious rescue fantasy. In order to support this conclusion, in the next section of this chapter we will report data that illustrates how he, in his open statements and actions, has linked Russia—as well as the image of the Soviet Union—to the time and place where his family lived surrounded by the Nazis, experienced many losses, and became preoccupied with burials and graveyards. Later we will describe Putin's role in malignant propaganda that aimed to rescue and protect Russia and its being a special place.

Time Collapse

In 2001 the "National Program of the Patriotic Education of Citizens of the Russian Federation" was created. Since then, it has been carried out by two five-year plans (Government of the Russian Federation, 2001; Government of the Russian Federation, 2015).

One of the aims of the program is to educate preschool-age kindergarten students about the Great Patriotic War, the Soviet name for World War II. In 2015 during the 70th anniversary of the victory in World War II, kindergartens and schools countrywide staged plays about this war. In many Russian towns, kindergartens and schools still stage and perform such plays.

These events typically start when a teacher, often dressed in the military uniform of the 1940s announces the beginning of the play and informs the participants that they will find themselves in the past. Following this, children, also dressed in clothes from the 1940s, have a good time dancing to one of the songs with the lyrics: "It's 1941 and everybody is alive." Suddenly music and dancing are interrupted by the voice of Yuri Levitan, the radio commentator who announced the start of the war back in 1941, usually using an authentic recording of his voice. After this announcement the children, now dressed in military uniforms from the 1940s, act out preparations "to go to the front" Next is a battle scene. Some children "die" and some pretend that they are graves. Those who "survive" come back home, celebrating "The Great Victory." (See www.youtube.com/watch?v= m2OM0v3wDIo for the illustration of a typical play).

At different locations there are some variations in these plays. For example, in some, background voices explain certain things that appear on the stage, such as the red blood of children on the white snow. In other plays, children approach their mothers and hand them papers symbolizing letters families received during World War II informing them that their children had been killed. Also, children play the role of soldiers who did not die in battle but find out when they return home that their mothers had died. At the end of the play children often state that they do not want war and that all they want is to live in peace. These plays are so widespread that the public can watch dozens of them on the internet. They are proudly uploaded by performers, parents, teachers, and administrators. Besides these "educational activities," dozens of plays by professional adults and movies "for children and their parents" are being dedicated to the Great Patriotic War. There is also a book, *Children's Book on War: Diaries* 1941–1945 (AiF, 2015) edited by a group of journalists from the newspaper *Argumenti i Fakti* (*Arguments and Facts*) owned by the Moscow government. Published in 2015, it includes stories of 35 Soviet children who experienced the atrocities of war. Tragic details, particularly related to the deaths of family members, especially from starvation in Leningrad, are described. It is not clear whether these diaries are authentic or not.

Wearing 1940s-style clothing has become very fashionable in Russia. Since 2017 modern military uniforms also have been replaced by military uniforms of the 1940s, now called "the winners'" uniforms. There are even military outfit stores for children, and they are very popular.

On May 9, the anniversary date of victory, the Russians have pompous parades besides the military ones. Big crowds take to the streets and march, carrying photos of their relatives who fought in World War II. Putin usually participates in the march called "Immortal Regiment" with a portrait of his father in his hands.

On November 29, 2015, when the 70th anniversary of the "Great Victory" was celebrated, the Russian Governmental TV channel Rossyia broadcast that the grave of Emperor Alexander III (father of Nicholas II—the last one killed by the Bolsheviks) had been opened in order to compare Alexander's remains with the existing remains of Nicholas II. It was important to learn that both belonged to the same family so they could be buried together along with Nicholas' children.

Normalization of necrophilia was observed in one Siberian town where a competition for grave digging took place. The Moscow Times (2020) published the story of this competition under the title: "Russian Gravediggers Defy

Coronavirus to Throw Speed-Digging Contest." Five teams from across the region descended upon a local cemetery to dig holes 2 meters long, 0.8 meters wide and 1.6 meters deep, with judges rating their performances. The winner was a young man from Tomsk who dug his grave in 52 minutes. Readers were informed that "new and more large-scale contests" will take place in the future.

Invasions

Before focusing on Putin's invasion of Ukraine, we will very briefly mention his involvement with other locations. Chechnya has struggled for independence since Russia invaded the North Caucasus in the 18th century. After the collapse of the Soviet Union, Chechnya declared independence (Chechen Republic of Ichkeria). Russian attempts failed during the early 1990s to regain control in Chechnya, in what became the 1994–1996 Russian–Chechen war. The unresolved Chechen issue was a challenge that Yeltsin handed to Putin. In 1999 Putin reinvaded Chechnya. This invasion was preceded by explosions at several buildings in various towns in Russia, attributed to "Chechen terrorists," though independent journalists wrote about their suspicions that Russian special forces caused these explosions (Eckel, 2019). Victory in this war became a "trademark" for Putin, as a strong leader who solved the Chechen issue.

Georgia was invaded by Russia for the first time at the beginning of the 19th century. In 1918 Georgia became independent while Russia was busy with its revolution, but on February 25, 1921, Georgia was reinvaded and endured 70 years of totalitarian regime. As soon as Georgia became independent again after the collapse of the Soviet Union, the Russian-fueled inter-ethnic political conflicts unfolded in its two regions—Abkhazia and Tskhinvali (South Ossetia). As a result, these two regions declared independence and up to 300,000 internally displaced people (IDP) fled to the rest of Georgia. The conflicts became protracted and in August 2008 developed into a five-day Russian–Georgian war. Following this war, Russia as well as its allies (Venezuela, Syria, Nicaragua, Nauru) recognized the independence of these breakaway regions. Since 2008, Putin has continued a so-called creeping occupation of Georgia by regularly moving the current "conflict border" (barbed wire) deeper and deeper into Georgia, in addition to other operations of a hybrid war (Bolkvadze et al., 2021).

As happened in Georgia, Ukraine suffered from Russian annexation since the 1920s. To suppress the resistance of the population, in 1932–1933 Soviet officials confiscated the entire grain supply from the population of the eastern and central villages of the country, closed the roads to restrict freedom of movement, and thus imposed an artificial famine which was named the Holodomor (Conquest, 1986; Marples, 2007). In Ukrainian, the word Holodomor means "to kill by starvation." Approximately 4.5 million people died during the Holodomor.

Since the collapse of the Soviet Union and Ukraine's regaining independence, choosing the political course for Euro-Atlantic integration has evolved in Ukraine. In 2013, after pro-Russian president Viktor Yanukovych suspended political association and free-trade agreements with the European Union, protests known as the Maidan Revolution rose up, and Yanukovych was ousted from office. In response, in 2014, Russia invaded Crimea and started a war in Donbas, and Russian-backed separatists declared independence in Lugansk and Donetsk, the two largest cities in Eastern Ukraine.

On February 24, 2022, Putin invaded Ukraine, which created massive numbers of forced internally displaced people and associated refugee problems. These millions of individuals, as well as a huge number of persons in host places and host countries, will face anxiety and confusion accompanied by large-group identity issues, mourning and adaptations, as well as many difficult real-life issues (Akhtar, 2014; Varvin, 2021; Volkan, 2017). Meanwhile, Putin and his propaganda machine continue to "justify" inhumane actions. The "delusional" aspect—the inflammation of the Nazi period of history—is clearly visible when Ukrainians are labeled Nazis. For example, on Russian television the Ukrainians are referred to as "Ukronazis" and the attack on Ukraine is linked to de-Nazification. On March 1, 2022, all Russian schools had to conduct special social sciences lessons to explain to children how they should think and talk about the so-called "special operation" in Ukraine; namely, they were taught to talk about it in terms of genocide and de-Nazification. To support these efforts, a propagandistic cartoon was produced and has been distributed widely (www.youtube.com/watch?v=oO3RY3Cv7Oc).

In one of his speeches after the invasion of Ukraine, Putin stated that the disintegration of our united country was brought about by the historical, strategic mistakes on the part of the Bolshevik leaders and the Communist Party of the Soviet Union (CPSU) leadership, mistakes committed at different times in state-building and economic and ethnic policies. The collapse of the historical Russia known as the USSR is on their conscience (Address by the President of Russian Federation, February 21, 2022, http://en.kremlin.ru/ events/president/news/67828).

Putin also has made many remarks illustrating his imitation of Joseph Stalin. Comparing himself, as well as competing with, Joseph Stalin calls to mind Putin's exaggerated self-narcissism. One wonders if he has a wish to be better known and more important than Stalin or other Soviet leaders.

Volkan (2004, 2013, 2020) has written about destructive narcissistic leaders' "glass bubble fantasies," their "living" in an isolated kingdom from which they watch others behind a glass enclosure and divide outsiders into two categories: those who adore them and those who do not. This plays a key role in how such a leader creates a severe political and societal division within his or her country and portrays another country as an enemy. In their own environment they hurt and sometimes destroy those who do not adore them. After the collapse of the Soviet Union, Volkan (1991a, 2013) interviewed Stalin's two private interpreters, Valentin Berezhkov and Zoya Zarubina. They told him stories about Stalin's private life, including how he burned people with his cigarette when he did not like their comments. In the clinical setting, we observe how an individual with a narcissistic personality organization responds to an event that threatens the person's grandiose self. He or she becomes anxious and intent upon finding new ways to protect the grandiose self. One wonders how COVID-19 might have threatened Putin's "First Person" identity.

Malignant Political Propaganda and Destructive Rescue Fantasy

When we first heard the news about the occupation of Ukraine, we recalled how after the collapse of the former Yugoslavia, Slobodan Milošević, with the help of some Serbian academicians and the Serbian Orthodox Church, re-enflamed the shared "memories" of the Serbian Battle of Kosovo that took place in 1389, the Serbian "chosen trauma." A chosen trauma is the shared mental image of an event in a large group's ancestors' history in which the large group suffered a catastrophic loss, humiliation, and helplessness at the hands of enemies, plus an inability to mourn these losses. The word "chosen" does not mean to imply that a large group "chooses" to be victimized by another large group and subsequently lose self-esteem. It does, however, recognize that the group "chooses" to psychologize and dwell on a past traumatic event and make it a major large-group identity marker, a chosen trauma or a chosen glory (Volkan, 1991b, 1997, 2013, 2014, 2019, 2020).

As the 600th anniversary of the Battle of Kosovo approached, the remains of the Serbian leader Prince Lazar who was killed during the Battle of Kosovo was removed from his grave in the north of Belgrade. The remains were placed in a coffin and taken over the course of the year from one Serbian town to another where they were received by huge crowds of mourners dressed in black. Again and again during this long journey, Lazar's remains were symbolically buried and reincarnated, until they were buried for good at the original battleground in Kosovo on June 28, 1989. Thus, Milošević and his associates, by activating the mental representations of Lazar and the Battle of Kosovo, along with the peak emotions they generated, first encouraged a shared sense of victimization followed by a shared sense of entitlement for revenge. This led to genocidal acts in Europe at the end of the 20th century.

When Milošević was 7, his favorite uncle, an army officer, put a gun to his head and killed himself. When Milošević was 21, his father did the same thing. His mother killed herself when he was in his early 30s. Milošević married his teenage sweetheart, Mirjana Milošević. Mirjana's mother, a

Yugoslav partisan during World War II, "was captured by the Nazis, tortured, surrendered crucial information, was released, and then was executed by the leader of her partisan group, who happened to be her father" (Mailer, 1999, p. A25).

Putin, like Milošević, had a background of traumas related to deaths and rescue fantasies. Milošević's interest in reincarnating Lazar's remains reminded us that Putin was a replacement child and of his investment in graveyards. Their similar political propaganda—short-lasting in Milošević's case and long-lasting in Putin's—are linked to the psychology of their internal worlds. Before them, Adolf Hitler (1925–1926) understood the power of political propaganda, devoting two chapters to its proper design and execution in *Mein Kampf*. To illustrate its aim he said, "The art of propaganda lies in understanding the emotional ideas of great masses and finding through a psychologically correct form, the way to attention and hence to the heart of the broad masses" (Hitler, 1925–1926, p. 180).

Volkan (2013) described seven steps of malignant propaganda. Both Milošević and Putin followed these steps.

The first step refers to enhancing a shared sense of victimization within the society by reactivating or inflaming a chosen trauma or a past shared undigested trauma. After the collapse of the Soviet Union and the independence of Estonia, Volkan and his interdisciplinary team conducted an unofficial diplomatic dialogue series that took place over several years between influential Estonians, people from Boris Yeltsin's government in Moscow, and leaders of Russian speakers in Estonia (Volkan, 1997, 2020). During these dialogue series, when Russian delegates from Moscow perceived a "threat" from Estonians, such as being disliked or considered "barbarous" by their former Soviet subjects, they would bring the mental representation of their chosen trauma to the negotiations, as resistance to listening sincerely to Estonians' concerns. The Russians' chosen trauma referred to their suffering at the hands of Tatars and Mongols in the 13th and 14th centuries. Putin, unlike Milošević, did not focus on a chosen trauma, but on an undigested trauma of the World War II period.

The second step is creating a time collapse that mixes up the image of a past "enemy" with the present devalued opposing large group, whether inside or outside the country. Above we described the time collapse in Russia.

The third step focuses on presenting the political leader as an omnipotent "savior" of his own large group while continuing to devalue the opposing large group and dehumanizing it.

The fourth step refers to elevating large-group identity to be more important than individual identity, through education in schools and other means. Below we will briefly describe what we mean by "large-group identity."

Personal identity provides an inner sense of persistent sameness for an individual (Erikson, 1956). Large-group identities are articulated in terms of commonality such as "we are Catalan; we are Lithuanian Jews; we are

Ukrainian, we are Sunni Muslim; we are communists, we are white supremacists in the United States." Large-group identities that develop in childhood are the end result of myths and realities of common beginnings, historical continuities, geographical realities, and shared linguistic, societal, religious, cultural, and ideological factors. Belonging to a large group is a natural phenomenon in human life.

Large-group identity also manifests when individuals are adults. Some religious cults and terrorist organizations truly represent large groups that evolve during adulthood. For members of religious cults or terrorist organizations, the investment in the core large-group identities that developed in childhood drastically changes. These individuals exaggerate selected aspects of their childhood large-group identities by holding on to a restricted special religious or nationalistic belief. Sometimes they become believers in ideas that were not available in their childhood environments. In short, they give up sharing overall sentiments with people who had the same core childhood large-group identity but who have not made their specific new selections.

The fifth step is to generalize a sense of "we-ness" (large-group narcissism) that is contaminated with an entitlement ideology; the members of the large group feel entitled to regain what their ancestors lost decades or centuries ago.

The Serbians' entitlement ideology is known in the literature as Christoslavism. Greeks call their entitlement ideology "Megali Idea" (Great Idea). In the United States there is a delusional entitlement ideology of White Supremacy.

Above, we wrote about the unofficial diplomatic dialogue series that took place in Estonia and how the suffering of Russians at the hands of Tatars and Mongols in the 13th and 14th centuries was remembered during these meetings. Referring to these events, a Russian delegate, a well-known person connected with the Russian government, began describing how Russia is entitled to occupy the lands of Others, but, unlike Tatars and Mongols of the 13th and 14th centuries, it would be a nice protector of Others. Addressing the Estonian delegates, he loudly declared that Estonians should not complain about being included in the Soviet Union. He stated that Russians are special people and they are the protectors of Estonia (Volkan, 1997, 2006). The present-day Russian entitlement ideology is to maintain "Russkiy Mir" (Russian World) as well as "Eurasionism" a position that Russian civilization does not belong in the usual "European" or "Asian" categories but instead to the larger geopolitical concept of Eurasia (Kudors, 2010).

The "Russkiy Mir" concept was elaborated upon by a group of Russian scholars (Pyotr Shchedrovitsky, Yefim Ostrovsky, Valery Tishkov, Vitaly Skrinnik, Tatyana Poloskova) in the 1990s in an attempt to respond to Russia's crisis of national ideology. Russkiy Mir assumes that the Russian

World is the social totality associated with language, traditions and history. According to the concept, Russia has a unique mission to protect Russkiy Mir in Russia and among compatriots abroad, meaning former Soviet people as well as Russian-speaking minorities. In 2007 Putin, co-operating with the Russian Orthodox Church, created the Russkiy Mir Foundation. The aim of this government-sponsored foundation is to promote the Russian language and culture worldwide and to form the Russian World as a global project (Kudors, 2010).

Another ideological concept that shapes a national idea of Putin's Russia and feeds entitlement ideology is related to Russian historian Lev Nikolayevich Gumilyov's (1912–1992) geopolitical concept called "Eurasianism" which tells us that Russian civilization is unique and special, and it does not belong in the European or Asian categories. According to Gumilyov (1990), the Russian ethnos is a "Super-ethnos," which has to oppose Catholic Europe's threat to Russia's integrity (Clover, 2016).

The sixth step of malignant political propaganda is creating a societal preoccupation with the large group's psychological borders through an obsession with physical borders, such as Putin's wish to expand present-day Russia's physical borders.

In the seventh step an entitlement ideology turns into dehumanizing the "enemy," revengeful actions, thus allowing mass killings and other inhumane actions to be committed.

The International Criminal Tribunal for the former Yugoslavia, a body of the United Nations, was created in 1993. The Tribunal tried Milošević on charges of 66 counts of crimes against humanity: genocide in Croatia, Bosnia, and Kosovo during the 1990s. Milošević conducted his own defense in the five-year trial which ended without a verdict. He died in prison in The Hague on March 11, 2006. We finished writing this chapter 50 days after the invasion of Ukraine began. We have no way to predict how this human tragedy will end and what Putin's future will be.

Note

1 This chapter is based on a paper that was given at the virtual conference "In the Time of War" of the *American Journal of Psychoanalysis*/Association for the Advancement of Psychoanalysis, on April 10, 2022, in response to the war in Ukraine. It then appeared in the *American Journal of Psychoanalysis* in June 2022.

References

Abend, S.M. (2008). Unconscious fantasy and modern conflict theory. *Psychoanalytic Inquiry*, 28, 117–130.

Akhtar, S. (2014). *Immigration and acculturation: Mourning, adaptation, and the next generation*. Rowman & Littlefield.

AiF. (2015). *Children's book on war—Diaries 1941–1945.* Arguments & Facts (in Russian).
Ainslie, R.C., & Solyom, A.E. (1986). The replacement of the fantasied Oedipal child: A disruptive effect of sibling loss on the mother-infant relationship. *Psychoanalytic Psychology,* 3, 257–268.
Arlow, J. A. (1969). Unconscious fantasy and disturbances of conscious experience. *Psychoanalytic Quarterly,* 38(1), 1–27.
Barry, E. (2012). At event, a rare look at Putin's life. *The New York Times,* January 28, 2012, Section A, p. 9.
Belton, C. (2020). *Putin's people: How the KGB took back Russia and then took on the West.* William Collins.
Beres, D. (1962). The unconscious fantasy. *Psychoanalytic Quarterly,* 31, 309–328.
Bergmann, M. S. (1973). Limitations of method in psychoanalytic biography: A historical inquiry. *Journal of the American Psychoanalytic Association,* 21(4), 833–850.
Bolkvadze, N., Chachava, K., Ghvedashvili, G., Lange-Ionatamis'vili, E., McMillan, J., Kalandarishvili, N., Keshelashvili, A., Kuprashvili, N., Sharashenidze, T. & Tsomaia, T. (2021). *Georgia's information environment through the lens of Russia's influence.* NATO Strategic Communications Centre of Excellence. https://Georgias-information-environment-through-the-lens-of-Russias-infulence.pdf
Cain, A.C., & Cain, B.S. (1964). On replacing a child. *Journal of the American Academy of Child Psychiatry,* 3, 443–456.
Clover, C. (2016). *Black wind, white snow: The rise of Russia's new nationalism.* Yale University Press.
Conquest, R. (1986). *The harvest of sorrow: Soviet collectivization and the terror-famine.* Oxford University Press.
Eckel, M. (2019). *Two decades on, smoldering questions about the Russian president's vault to power.* Radio Liberty.
Erikson, E.H. (1956). The problem of ego identity. *Journal of the American Psychoanalytic Association,* 4, 56–121.
Erikson, E.H. (1958). *Young man Luther.* Norton.
Government of the Russian Federation Resolution no. 1493, December 30, 2015, "Patriotic education of citizens of Russian Federation for 2016–2020."
Government of the Russian Federation Program "Patriotic education of citizens of Russian Federation for 2001–2005," Moscow 2001. Retrieved on April 20, 2022, from www.ainros.ru/ssylki/patr_vos.html
Green, N., & Solnit, A.J. (1964). Reactions to the threatened loss of a child: A vulnerable child syndrome. *Pediatrics,* 34(1), 58–66.
Gumilyov, L. (1990). *Ethnogenesis and the biosphere.* Progress.
Hamilton, H. (1969). Object loss, dreaming and creativity: The poetry of John Keats. *Psychoanalytic Study of the Child,* 24(1), 488–531.
Hamilton, H. (1979). Joseph Conrad: His development as an artist, 1889–1910. *Psychoanalytic Study of Society,* 34, 277–329.
Hitler, A. (1925–1926). *Mein Kampf [My Struggle].* Houghton Mifflin.
Ikle, F.C. (1971). *Every war must end.* Columbia University Press.
Inderbitzin, L.B., & Levy, S.T. (1990). Unconscious fantasy: A reconsideration of the concept. *Journal of the American Psychoanalytic Association,* 38(1), 113–130.

Javakhishvili, J.D. (2014). Soviet legacy in contemporary Georgia: A psychotraumatological perspective. *Identity Studies*, 5, 20–40.
Javakhishvili, J. D. (2018). Trauma caused by the repressions of totalitarian regime in Georgia and its transgenerational transmission. Doctoral Dissertation.
Kestenberg, J.S., & Brenner, I. (1996). *The last witness*. American Psychiatric Press.
Kogan, I. (1995). *The cry of mute children: A psychoanalytic perspective of the second generation of the Holocaust*. London: Free Association Books.
Kudors, A. (2010). Russian World: Russia's soft power approach to compatriots' policy. *Russian Analytical Digest*, 81(10), 2–4.
Laub, D., & Auerhahn, N.C. (1993). Knowing and not knowing massive psychic trauma: Forms of traumatic memory. *International Journal of Psycho-Analysis*, 74(2), 287–302.
Legg, C., & Sherick, I. (1976). The replacement child—A developmental tragedy: Some preliminary comments. *Child Psychiatry and Human Development*, 7(2), 113–126.
Mailer, N. (1999). Milošević and Clinton. *The Washington Post*, May 24, p. A25.
Malkin, E., & Zhahor, Z. (1992). *Leaders and leadership: Collected essays*. Zlaman Shezar Center and Israeli Historical Society (in Hebrew).
Marples, D.R. (2007). *Heroes and villains: Creating national history in contemporary Ukraine*. Central European University Press.
The Moscow Times. (2020). Russian gravediggers defy coronavirus to throw speed-digging contest. *The Moscow Times*, April 14, 2022.
Myers, S.L. (2015). *The new tsar: The rise and reign of Vladimir Putin*. Albert A. Knopf.
Olinick, S.L. (1980). *The psychotherapeutic instrument*. Jason Aronson.
Plank, E. M., & Plank, R. (1978). Children and death: As seen through art and autobiographies. *Psychoanalytic Study of the Child*, 33(1), 593–620.
Pollock, G. (1975). On mourning, immortality, and Utopia. *Journal of the American Psychoanalytic Association*, 23(2), 334–362.
Poznanski, E.O. (1972). The "replacement child": A saga of unresolved parental grief. *Behavioral Pediatrics*, 81(6), 1190–1193.
Putin, V. (2015). Life is such a simple thing and cruel. *Russian Pioneer*, 55.
Putin, V., Gevorkyan, N., Timakova, N., & Kolesnikov, A. (2000). *First person: An astonishingly frank self-portrait by Russia's president Vladimir Putin*. C. A. Fitzpatrick (Trans.). Public Affairs.
Reid, A. (2011). *Leningrad: The epic siege of World War II, 1941–1944*. Walker Books.
Roxburgh, A. (2013). *The strongman: Vladimir Putin and the struggle for Russia*. I.B. Tauris.
Schmidt-Löw-Beer, C., Atria, M., & Davar, E. (2015). Communism and the trauma of its collapse. *American Journal of Psychoanalysis*, 75, 394–415.
Varvin, S. (2021). *Psychoanalysis in social and cultural settings: Upheavals and resilience*. Routledge.
Volkan, V.D. (1981). Linking objects and linking phenomena: A study of the forms, symptoms, metapsychology and therapy of complicated mourning. International Universities Press.
Volkan, V.D. (1991a). An interview with Valentin Berezhkov: Stalin's interpreter. *Mind & Human Interaction*, 2, 77–80.

Volkan, V.D. (1991b). On chosen trauma. *Mind and Human Interaction*, 3, 13.
Volkan, V.D. (1997). *Bloodlines: From ethnic pride to ethnic terrorism*. Farrar, Straus, and Giroux.
Volkan, V.D. (2004). *Blind trust: Large groups and their leaders in times of crises and terror*. Pitchstone.
Volkan, V.D. (2006). *Killing in the name of identity: A study of bloody conflicts*. Pitchstone.
Volkan, V.D. (2010). *Psychoanalytic technique expanded: A textbook on psychoanalytic treatment*. Oa Press.
Volkan, V.D. (2013). *Enemies on the couch: A psychopolitical journey through war and peace*. Pitchstone.
Volkan, V.D. (2014). *Psychoanalysis, international relations, and diplomacy: A sourcebook on large-group psychology*. Karnac.
Volkan, V.D. (2017). *Immigrants and refugees: Trauma, perennial mourning, and border psychology*. Karnac.
Volkan, V.D. (2019). Large-group identity. Who are we now? Leader-follower relationships and societal-political divisions. *American Journal of Psychoanalysis*, 79, 139–155.
Volkan, V.D. (2020). *Large-group psychology: Racism, societal divisions, narcissistic leaders and who we are now?* Phoenix.
Volkan, V.D., Akhtar, S., Dorn, R.M., Kafka, J.S., Kernberg, O.F., Olsson, P.A., Rogers, R.R., & Shanfield, S. (1998). Psychodynamics of leaders and decision-making. *Mind and Human Interaction*, 9, 129–181.
Volkan, V.D., & Ast, G. (1997). *Siblings in the unconscious and psychopathology*. International Universities Press.
Volkan, V.D., & Itzkowitz, N. (1984). *The immortal Atatürk: A psychobiography*. University of Chicago Press.
Volkan, V.D., Itzkowitz, N., & Dod, A. (1997). *Richard Nixon: A psychobiography*. Columbia University Press.
von Rochau, A.L. (1853). Grundsätze der Realpolitik, angewendet auf die Zustände Deutschlands [*Principles of realpolitik, applied to the state of Germany*]. Ullstein.
Wolfenstein, M. (1973). The image of the lost parent. *Psychoanalytic Study of the Child*, 28(1), 433–456.

PART 4

Quantitative Research Conducted by a Preeminent Researcher

Chapter 6

Measuring the Mental Functioning of Putin, Trump, and Zelensky

Robert M. Gordon

History informs us that the malignant mental illness of autocratic leaders causes the worst avoidable suffering. It is the duty of experts to educate and warn of such dangers.

One objective way to do so is to consider a person's capacity for mature leadership by assessing: the weight of evidence, insightfulness, communication skills, the ability to make rational and realistic decisions, high stress tolerance, resiliency and adaptation, good impulse control, and healthy standards and ideals. The Psychodiagnostic Chart (PDC-2) is the assessment tool of the Psychodynamic Diagnostic Manual (PDM-2). The PDC-2's Mental Functioning scales were used in this study since they show a high degree of utility for measuring these mental traits and are useful for informing the voting public.

To test the utility of the Mental Function scales we used a purposive group of 50 mental health experts to rate Vladimir Putin, Donald Trump, and Volodymyr Zelensky.

This study demonstrated that the PDC-2's Mental Functioning scale was sensitive to both large and subtle differences in these political leaders. The Mental Functioning scale measured Volodymyr Zelensky with an overall 91 percent. This indicates a psychologically healthy leader. Vladimir Putin's average score was 41 percent which is in the severe mental illness range. Donald Trump was rated at the 25 percent level of Mental Functioning or in the severe mental illness range. Putin and Trump both scored in the dangerous range in all 12 Mental Functions.

In just 43 years, from 1933 to 1976, an estimated 190 million people died due to the leadership of only three men: Adolf Hitler, Joseph Stalin, and Mao Zedong (Gordon, 2022). They all claimed to protect their citizens from the dangers created by their own delusional megalomania and paranoias. They used fear-mongering, scapegoating, and blame-shifting (Messina, 2022). Hitler was at first installed as chancellor to fight communism during Germany's severe economic crisis and humiliating post-war reparations. The United States and many of the capitalist nations at that time were also more concerned about the threat of communism than of fascism.

DOI: 10.4324/9781032637822-11

Fascism might be the toxin to communism, but it is equally poisonous to a liberal democracy.

Social scientists believe that we evolved a tendency to follow an idealized charismatic alpha male, even to our self-destruction. This idealization is increased by peoples' feelings of insecurity and fear. Personality traits are also predictive of who supports an authoritarian leader. Xu and Plaks (2022) in their study of 1,257 voters in the 2016 and 2020 US presidential elections, using a well-validated personality test, the Big 5, found that Trump supporters scored lower in Open Mindedness and Compassion and had the lowest education level compared to both Clinton and Biden supporters. Being more closed-minded and less educated makes a person more vulnerable to manipulation by propaganda and conspiracy theories, which are used to full effect by authoritarian populists.

The idealization of an authoritarian populist can be as enduring as any religious myth. Although it is estimated that Stalin may have killed from 40 million to 60 million of his own people, a record 70 percent of Russian respondents said that he played a positive role for Russia, according to a 2019 poll by the independent Moscow-based Levada Center.

From 1958 to 1962, Mao Zedong's Great Leap Forward policy led to the deaths of up to 45 million Chinese. Mao's level of empathy is apparent in his statement: "When there is not enough to eat, people starve to death. It is better to let half the people die so that others can eat their fill." Yet a 2013 Global Times Poll Center survey of 1,045 respondents in China revealed that more than 90 percent of respondents have reverence for Mao.

The Nazis under Hitler killed about 30 million men, women, handicapped, aged, sick, prisoners of war, forced laborers, camp inmates, critics, homosexuals, Jews, Slavs, Serbs, Germans, Czechs, Italians, Poles, French, Ukrainians, and others. Donald Trump is apparently an admirer of Hitler. During his presidency he told John Kelly, then his chief of staff and a retired Marine Corps general, that he wanted "totally loyal" generals like the ones who had served Adolf Hitler (Baker & Glasser, 2022). When Kelly reminded Trump that Hitler was our enemy in World War II, Donald Trump said to John Kelly: "Well, Hitler did a lot of good things" (Bender, 2021).

Baker and Glasser also reported that Kelly bought a copy of Dr. Bandy Lee's 2017 book entitled, *The Dangerous Case of Donald Trump*. In it, 37 mental health professionals warned that Trump was psychologically unfit for office. Kelly used Lee's book as a guide in his attempts to cope with Trump's irrational behavior.

Edwards and Rushin (2018) using time series analysis, showed that Trump's election in November of 2016 was associated with a statistically significant surge in reported hate crimes across the United States, even when controlling for alternative explanations. Further, by using panel regression techniques, they showed that counties that voted for Trump by the widest margins also experienced the largest increases in reported hate crimes.

Feinberg, Branton, and Martinez-Ebers (2022) also find that counties that hosted Trump rallies experienced an increase in hate-motivated events.

Woodward and Costa (2021) reported that General Mark Milley, chairman of the Joint Chiefs of Staff, feared that Donald Trump might go "rogue" and launch a nuclear war or an attack on China after Trump lost the 2020 election and had incited insurrection. Milley called General Li Zuocheng, chief of the Joint Staff of the People's Liberation Army of China to reassure him that they were safe from Trump. Milley also thought that Trump was treasonous since he tried to overthrow the government to stay in power.

Yet, the twice-impeached Trump got about 47 percent of the vote in the 2020 election and still has a strong following.

It is estimated that Vladimir Putin had 82 journalists and media people murdered, as reported by the Committee to Protect Journalists. Putin has imprisoned and had murdered anyone he considered a threat to his power. In February of 2022, Putin launched a brutal unprovoked invasion of Ukraine, starting the first major war in Europe since World War II. On March 16, 2022, President Joseph Biden called Putin "a war criminal" due to his policy of leveling cities and targeting civilians. Putin's view of free speech was evident on that same day when in a televised speech in reference to the Russian war protesters he said,

> the Russian people, will always be able to distinguish the true patriots from the scum and the traitors, and just to spit them out like a midge that accidentally flew into their mouths ... I am convinced that this natural and necessary self-cleansing of society ...

The Ukrainian General Staff (UGS) published images on September 16, 2022, showing several mass burial sites with civilian bodies that showed signs of torture and brutality in locations that had been occupied by Russian forces.

After Putin annexed parts of the Ukraine, his paranoia was evident in his annexation speech on September 30, 2022, in which he described the West as "a radical denial of moral norms, religion, and family ... is directed against all societies ... the overthrow of faith and traditional values ... outright Satanism."

When Vladimir Putin invaded the Ukraine in February of 2022, Trump stated, "You gotta say, that's pretty savvy ... This is genius ... Putin declares a big portion of the Ukraine ... Oh, that's wonderful."

The greatest share of avoidable human suffering has been caused by irrational authoritarian leaders. We have yet to have find a way to help prevent such tragedy, other than having an active objective news media and upholding the rule of law in liberal democracies. Both the media and the courts have relied on expert opinion. The expert opinion on the psychological fitness for office may be one of our most important safeguards.

Torre (1970) called for safeguards in political systems to protect against irrational leaders. He noted that qualifying mental capacity evaluations are common for lower-level government positions but not for leadership positions. He argued that prior to election, mental capacity evaluations should be a prerequisite for candidacy.

However, it is unlikely that political candidates would agree to such an examination, or if they did, the findings are not likely to be valid. Candidates for office are often experts in presenting an idealized image of themselves. They would certainly be coached in how to fake looking good. Also, research on the effectiveness of interviews for someone motivated to fake looking good is often inferior to records reviews and observer ratings (Dana, Dawes & Peterson, 2013). This is especially true for those with psychopathic traits who are naturally skilled at deception (Bodholdt, 2000).

It is possible to evaluate political candidates' personalities based on their documented statements and recorded observed behaviors, in the same manner that forensic psychologists formulate and offer their evaluations to law enforcement or to the courts when they are not able to directly test an individual. Expert mental health professionals can apply a valid methodology and offer their assessment of political candidates and leaders to help educate the public as to their mental fitness for office.

Scientific research supports the validity of experts rating politicians' personality traits regarding leadership quality.

The most common expert rating assessments for studying leadership traits are the Five Factor Measures, also known as the Big Five, or NEO. The five factors are: Openness to Experience (open-minded), Conscientiousness, Extraversion, Agreeableness, Neuroticism (general psychopathology) (McCrae & Costa, 1985). These measures are practical for research since they are short and easy to interpret.

Rice, Remmel, and Mondak (2021) used the Big Five trait ratings for 87 United States senators provided by US Senate insiders. Rubenzer and Faschingbauer (2004) had 115 experts who were biographers, historians, and presidential advisers rate all the US presidents based mainly on the Revised NEO Personality Inventory (NEO PI-R), which is a form of the five-factor model and its subscales. They reported that presidential success was most correlated with: Assertiveness (.37), Tender Mindedness (.34), Achievement Striving (.32), Intellectual Brilliance (.30), and Activity (.30). Simonton (2002) studied presidents and found intelligence to be a significant factor that contributes to performance. Since IQ is positively correlated to Openness to Experience (Bartels et al., 2012), it would be expected to find that they are both be related to presidential success.

Nai and Toros (2020) compared the Big Five and the D12 Inventory for the Dark Triad (i.e., Narcissism, Psychopathy, and Machiavellianism; Jones & Paulhus, 2014) scores of 157 world leaders between June 2016 and July 2019. Using the ratings provided by more than 1,800 scholars, they found that "Candidates identified as 'autocrats' score significantly higher than non-autocrats on the three traits of the Dark Triad, and especially psychopathy" (p. 16). Trump had the highest score in Extraversion, and the lowest scores on Agreeableness, Conscientiousness, and Emotional stability. On the Dark Triad, both Putin and Trump scored very high on Psychopathy with Trump having the highest scores on Narcissism and Machiavellianism—and the second-highest score on Psychopathy.

Similar to the Big Five is the HEXACO which has six-factor traits, with the addition of the Honest-Humility factor (Ashton & Lee, 2007). The six personality traits are: Honest-Humility, Emotionality, Extraversion, Agreeableness, Conscientiousness, and Openness to Experience. Research into leadership indicates that the addition of the Honest-Humility factor is a valuable contribution. The Honest-Humility factor was related inversely to a wide array of criteria, including criminal activity and other unethical behaviors as well as materialistic and power-seeking tendencies (Ashton & Lee, 2007). "Honesty-Humility is essentially equivalent (at its opposite pole) to the common element shared by the Dark Triad" (i.e., Narcissism, Psychopathy, and Machiavellianism) (Lee & Ashton, 2005, 2014). Jonason and McCain (2012) also found that HEXACO's Honest-Humility factor was strongly inversely related to the Dark Triad. Visser, Book and Volk (2017) had ten personality assessment experts use the HEXACO and found Trump's scores were very low on Honesty-humility, Emotionality-Altruism, Agreeableness, Conscientiousness, and Openness to Experience, but high on Extraversion.

While both the five- and six-factor personality assessments proved useful in the research on leadership qualities, the number of traits is too few to have much practical utility in deciding between political candidates. For example, both the Big Five and the HEXACO have only one scale, Neuroticism, to assess the vast array of mental disorders. Their lack of subtly and complexity is likely because the creation of the five- or six-trait taxonomies was based on using conscious language descriptions that were then mathematically (by factor analysis) put into the five or six factors. They are not derived from any theory of development or personality. They are mathematical artifacts.

The personality of leaders and their success is complex. For example, Kowert (1996) using the five factors, found a complex relationship between presidential greatness and personality. Their data provided little support for the hypothesis that a president's personality is related to his overall "greatness" rating by historians on just the five factors. However, presidents rated high on Openness and did better in policy deliberations during international crises.

The D12 Inventory for the Dark Triad (i.e., Narcissism, Psychopathy, and Machiavellianism), in contrast to the factor-derived scales, is backed by a theory of personality. This D12 inventory is more useful in warning about destructive candidates than the tests based on just five or six factors. However, learning that a leader has psychopathic traits may not weaken support. It is likely that many conservatives can acknowledge Trump's personality flaws and justify their support for Trump as a pragmatic choice to achieve their political goals.

McBride (2021) reported that 81 percent of white American Evangelicals voted for Trump, even though he embodied moral values they deemed repugnant, but considered him a messianic figure, akin to King David, supposedly anointed by God despite his immoral behavior. McBride, however, argues that Evangelicals supported Trump because they resonate with his authoritarian values.

Some Trump supporters upon learning that Trump is a psychopath might see it as a positive trait signifying that he can get things done (McDermott, 2020). Trump intuitively understood this when he said in January of 2016 while running for president, "I could stand in the middle of 5th Avenue and shoot somebody, and I wouldn't lose voters."

The Psychodynamic Diagnostic Manual 2 and the Psychodiagnostics Chart 2 (PDC-2)

The assessment of personality is difficult, and assessing a mature and effective leader is particularly difficult. There is a need for a more useful assessment of fitness for office that takes account of this complexity. Such an assessment also needs to communicate both the strengths and weaknesses of a person rather than just a psychiatric diagnosis. The American Psychiatric Association's diagnostic classification system or the Diagnostic and Statistical Manuals are basically taxonomies of descriptive psychiatry. These manuals describe symptoms. The International Classification of Diseases similarly describes mental disorders. The Psychodynamic Diagnostic Manuals (PDM) were published in 2006 (Gordon, 2010) and updated in 2017, with the goal of better understanding the whole of personality, including a person's weaknesses and strengths. Based on psychodynamic theory and research, the PDM encompassed many levels of personality and not just a description of mental illness symptoms. The PDM also had sections that were sensitive to personality development throughout a life span.

The Psychodiagnostic Chart (PDC) was developed in 2012 by Robert M. Gordon and Robert F. Borstein to codify the highly complex PDM. They later updated it (Gordon & Bornstein, 2018) for the PDM-2 (Lingiardi & McWilliams, 2017). The PDC-2 is a quick practitioner rating form that may be used for diagnoses, treatment formulations, progress reports, and outcome assessments, as well as for empirical research on personality. It can be used when the subject is not available, and assessment is instead based on documents, records, collateral interviews, or other sources of information. Research by Gordon and Stoffey (2014) and Gordon and

Bornstein (2018) show excellent validity of the original PDC and updated PDC-2. Additionally, several other studies support the clinical utility and validity of the PDC-2 (https://sites.google.com/site/psychodiagnosticchart/). Copies of the PDC-2 are also available free on that website.

The PDC-2 assesses:

- Level of Personality Organization (Healthy, Neurotic, Borderline, or Psychotic). The PDM-2 describes the Level of Personality Organization thus:

   At the healthy end ... they can engage in satisfying relationships, experience and understand a relatively full range of age-expected feelings and thoughts, function with relative flexibly when stressed by external or internal conflict, maintain a relatively coherent sense of personal identity, express impulses in a manner appropriate to the situation, conduct themselves in accordance with internalized moral values, and neither suffer undue distress or impose it on others.

   (pp. 17–18)

- 12 Personality Syndromes (P-Axis: Depressive, Dependent, Anxious, Obsessive-Compulsive, Schizoid, Somatizing, Hysteric-Histrionic, Narcissistic, Paranoid, Psychopathic, Sadistic, Borderline)
- 12 Mental Functioning Items (M-Axis):

   1 Capacity for regulation, attention, and learning
   2 Capacity for affective range, communication, and understanding
   3 Capacity for mentalization and reflective functioning
   4 Capacity for differentiation and integration (identity)
   5 Capacity for relationships and intimacy
   6 Capacity for self-esteem regulation and quality of internal experience
   7 Capacity for impulse control and regulation
   8 Capacity for defensive functioning
   9 Capacity for adaptation, resiliency, and strength
   10 Self-observing capacities (psychological mindedness)
   11 Capacity to construct and use internal standards and ideals
   12 Capacity for meaning and purpose

- The S-Axis, which reflects a person's subjective symptoms (anxiety, depression, etc.)
- Context and Cultural Factors affecting a person's condition.

New Research on the Utility of the Mental Functioning Scale for Assessing Fitness for Office

For this study, we used a purposive group of expert raters. A purposive sampling is used when the experiment calls for a special non-random group, such as a select group of experts. Our experts were recruited from the listserv of the Society for Psychoanalysis and Psychoanalytic Psychology and the listserv of the American Psychoanalytic Association. The members of these groups would be familiar with the complex psychodynamic constructs used in the PDC-2 as compared to mental health experts from other theoretical orientations.

Before–we recruited our experts, the Washington-Baltimore Center for Psychoanalysis' Institutional Review Board found that there is expected to be no harm to participants with this online survey research.

The request posted on the listservs asked for mental health experts to be able to use the Psychodynamic Diagnostic Manual-2's PDC-2 to rate Trump, Putin, and Zelensky. The post also suggested:

You may read about these men on Wikipedia, and then rate them.

https://en.wikipedia.org/wiki/Donald_Trump

https://en.wikipedia.org/wiki/Vladimir_Putin

https://en.wikipedia.org/wiki/Volodymyr_Zelenskyy

Respondents were asked, in addition to agreeing to the Informed Consent, to attest that they have no conflict of interest that would significantly impair their objectivity, competence, or effectiveness.

Fifty mental health experts completed the survey online in September of 2022. All the respondents agreed to the Informed Consent at the beginning of the survey. Most respondents were older mental health professionals of 65 or more years of age (64 percent). Fifty percent identified as male, 50 percent identified as female, and none as non-binary or other. Eighty-six percent responded as White, 6 percent as Hispanic, 4 percent as Asian, and 4 percent as Black. Eighty-two percent stated that they had doctoral degrees, and 18 percent had master's degrees. Most were licensed as psychologists (55 percent), followed by psychiatrists (27 percent), social workers (10 percent), and counselors (8 percent). Respondents were asked about their political orientation (1 = Left, 5 = Moderate, 9 = Right; N = 49, 47 percent of the sample were in the moderate range between 4–6, $M = 3.55$, $SD = 1.31$).

Materials and Procedure

This study explores the utility of the M-Axis of Mental Functions of the PDC-2, which assesses psychological strengths and weaknesses of a person. The M-Axis does not offer a definitive mental disorder diagnosis and thereby avoids the problem of the "Goldwater Rule" for some psychiatrists (I say "some" since most psychiatrists consider the 1973 "rule" as obsolete.)

Also, the total Mental Functioning score can be converted to a simple percentage score that is easily understood without psychological jargon, similar to a grade (i.e., the total Mental Functioning score/total possible score).

The 50 experts were asked to rate each item on this scale: 1 = Severe Defects, 2 = Major Impairments, 3 = Moderate Impairments, 4 = Mild Impairments, 5 = Healthy.

The 12 items of the Mental Functioning scale are:

1 Capacity for regulation, attention, and learning includes the capacity to attend to and process information, focus, and learn from experience.
2 Capacity for affective range, communication, and understanding includes the capacity to experience, express, and comprehend the full range of emotions in ways that are appropriate for a particular situation and consistent with cultural norms.
3 Capacity for mentalization and reflective functioning includes the capacity to understand and interpret the behavior of self and others in terms of mental states (e.g., needs, desires, feelings, beliefs, goals, intentions, and motivations), and ability to take another person's perspective.
4 Capacity for differentiation and integration (identity) includes the capacity to distinguish self from other, fantasy from reality, internal representations from external objects and present from past and future and to construct and maintain a differentiated, realistic, coherent, complex representation of self (identity).
5 Capacity for relationships and intimacy includes the capacity for intimacy and connectedness that reflects the depth, range, and stability required for mutually satisfying relationships.
6 Capacity for self-esteem regulation and quality of internal experience includes the capacity for self-esteem regulation and stability, with self-confidence and self-esteem based on reality-based perceptions, being neither unrealistically high nor unrealistically low.
7 Capacity for impulse control and regulation includes the capacity to modulate impulses and express them in adaptive, culture-appropriate ways without either unmodulated expression of impulses or rigid over-control of impulses (inhibition).
8 Capacity for defensive functioning includes the capacity to modulate anxiety, or threat to self-esteem without excessive distortion in self-perception and reality testing, and without making excessive use of denial, projection, splitting, idealization/devaluation, or acting out.
9 Capacity for adaptation, resiliency, and strength includes the capacity to adjust to unexpected events and changing circumstances, and the ability to cope effectively and creatively when confronted with uncertainty, loss, stress, and challenge.

10 Self-observing capacities (psychological mindedness) include the individual's ability to observe his or her own internal life mindfully and realistically and use this information adaptively to facilitate self-awareness.
11 Capacity to construct and use internal standards and ideals includes the capacity to formulate values, standards and ideals and the ability to make mindful decisions based on a set of coherent, flexible, and internally consistent underlying moral principles.
12 Capacity for meaning and purpose includes the capacity for directedness and purpose, a concern for succeeding generations, and a spirituality (not necessarily expressed as traditional religiosity) that imbues one's life with meaning.

As you can see, these 12 Mental Functioning items use understandable language, but it takes an expert in psychodynamic personality assessment to rate someone accurately. We focused on the PDC-2's Mental Functioning section for this study, since in many cases a definitive mental disorder diagnosis may not be applicable or as useful as understanding a person's complex Mental Functioning. The Mental Functioning scale gives us a measure of a continuum of strengths and weaknesses on a full array of all the main psychological functions. However, there will be cases where a personality disorder (such as malignant narcissism or psychopathy) may also be helpful (as in the case of Trump or Putin), and the full PDC-2 (and Dark Triad scale) can be used for that as well.

To test how well the Mental Functioning scales work in assessing candidates for national office, we chose to compare three well-known political leaders whose actions have been frequently in the current news. We asked mental health experts to rate Donald Trump (US president from 2017–2021), Vladimir Putin (president of Russia since 2012, having previously served between 2000 and 2008), and Volodymyr Zelensky (current president of Ukraine since 2019).

Overall, Trump and Putin have poor ratings as leaders, and Zelensky generally has high ratings. A 2019 Global Pew Research Center poll of confidence in German Chancellor Angela Merkel, Emmanuel Macron, Vladimir Putin, Donald Trump, and Xi Jinping showed that Merkel got the most positive rating of 46 percent. Trump received 29 percent positive ratings—similar to the confidence in Chinese President Xi Jinping (28 percent). However, 64 percent of people polled express *no confidence* in Trump which is higher than it is for all the other world leaders asked about.

A March 2022 Pew Research Center poll found that 72 percent of Americans had confidence in Zelensky's handling of international affairs, while Putin received only 6 percent of US adults expressing confidence in him (www.pewresearch.org/topic/politics).

In this study we asked 50 mental health professionals to rate Trump, Putin, and Zelensky according to the PDC-2 M-Axis items to assess the utility of the PDC-2 for better understanding the mental qualities of future political candidates, and to develop a simple metric for informing the voter.

We hypothesized that the overall Mental Functioning score should be much higher for Zelensky than for Trump or Putin. We expected both Trump and Putin to score very low on the Mental Functioning scale, with Putin scoring slightly higher than Trump.

Results

The PDC-2's 12 Mental Functioning items (with scores ranging from: 1 = Severe Defects, to 5 = Healthy), showed Zelensky as consistently "Healthy" across all the 12 Mental Functions ($M = 4.57$, $SD = .77$, overall percentage, 4.47/5 = 91 percent).

Both Putin and Trump scored in the severely mentally disordered range in all 12 Mental Functions. Putin's average score was ($M = 2.04$, $SD = 1.06$, 41 percent) or in the "Major Impairments" range of functioning. Trump's average score was ($M = 1.25$, $SD = .61$, 25 percent) or "Severe Defects" range of Mental Functioning. Trump scored significantly lower than Putin in all of the 12 Mental Functions (all two-tailed, $p < .001$). See Table 6.1.

The smallest difference between Trump and Putin was on M12-Capacity for meaning and purpose, including the capacity for directedness and purpose, a concern for succeeding generations, and a spirituality (not necessarily expressed as traditional religiosity) that imbues one's life with meaning. Putin was rated $M = 1.82$, $SD = 1.19$, and Trump was rated $M = 1.29$, $SD = .63$ ($t = -3.53$, $df = 44$, $p < .001$).

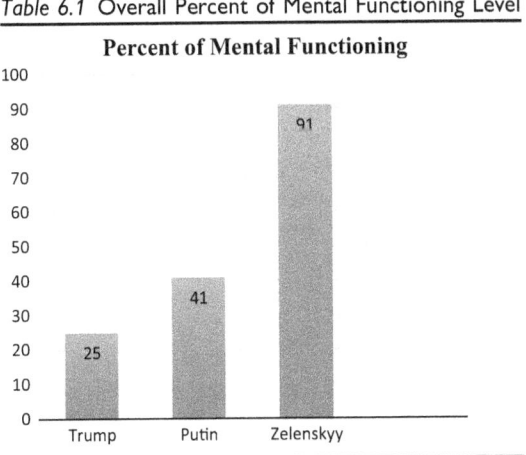

Table 6.1 Overall Percent of Mental Functioning Level

In other words, both men similarly have extreme selfish, amoral values consistent with a psychopathic personality. Note that on the 1 to 5 scale, they are both rated in the 1–2 psychotic level range (Severe Defects–Major Impairments).

The largest difference between Trump and Putin was on M1-Capacity for regulation, attention, and learning that includes the capacity to attend to and process information, to focus, and to learn from experience. Putin was rated $M = 2.96$, $SD = 1.21$, or "Moderate Impairments" and Trump was rated $M = 1.47$, $SD = .86$ ($t = -8.29$, $df = 46$, $p < .001$) or in the "Severe Defects" functioning range. In other words, while acknowledging that both men do not learn well from their mistakes because of their pathological defenses, Trump is perceived as lacking rational intelligence.

Thus, the PDC-2 Mental Functioning scale performed as hypothesized. It was able to show both the very large differences between Zelensky and Trump and Putin, as well as sensitivity to the subtle differences between Putin and Trump.

The political orientation of the raters had very little effect on their ratings. There were no significant correlations between the raters' political orientation and their assessments of Trump, Putin, and Zelensky. The correlations between political orientation and Mental Functioning rating ranged from Trump's Internal Standards and Ideals (where r was .00) to Putin's Relationships and Intimacy (where r was .31).

The low, non-significant correlations might have been the result of our instructions to the expert raters to score according to their professional ethics, that is trying to be aware of and to minimize bias. Mental health professionals often must assess and treat clients who may greatly differ from their personal values and beliefs.

Discussion

In this study we use a "purposive sampling" of mental health experts. By purposive sampling (or selective sampling) we decided that the most valid methodology was by choosing mental health experts to rate political figures on a well-validated psychological test. In this sample of licensed mental health professionals, we found no significant political bias in their ratings. All people are politically biased to some degree. However, the professional ethics of mental health professionals require them to be aware of their biases and to find ways to minimize their interference in their professional judgments. Mental health professionals are often required to diagnose and treat people with whom they have different political and religious views and are accustomed to temporally putting aside their biases in doing their professional work. Professional ethics, self-awareness and especially the use of objective assessments help to control for biases (Greiffenstein et al., 2010; Meyer et al., 2001).

Murray and Blessing (2010) in their survey of almost 1,000 professional historians on what constitutes a successful performance in the presidency found that conservative and liberal historians show considerable overall agreement in their ratings despite expected biases.

Visser, Book and Volk (2018) used ten personality assessment experts to rate Hilary Clinton and Donald Trump on the HEXACO scales. They realized that their academic sample would be more liberal than the general public; however, they found no significant bias,

> ... [W]e emphasized that they were to conduct an objective evaluation on each candidate's personality ... objectivity is a crucial part of a scientist's job that is closely scrutinized under peer-review ... there was no reason to believe that our professionals would behave any less objectively with our work than in their own.
>
> (p. 7)

Ethical Issues

Psychiatrists have a "Goldwater Rule," which requires an examination and proper authorization. However, in this study psychiatrists were not asked to name a definitive psychiatric disorder. Also, the "Goldwater Rule" as Lilienfeld, Miller and Lynam (2018) concluded,

> ... is outdated and premised on dubious scientific assumptions. We further contend that there are select cases in which psychological scientists with suitable expertise may harbor a 'duty to inform,' allowing them to offer informed opinions concerning public figures' mental health with appropriate caveats.
>
> (p. 3)

All other licensed mental health professionals do not have an equivalent "Goldwater Rule," but are required to form conclusions based on scientific standards. The American Psychological Association (2016) *Ethical Principles of Psychologists and Code of Conduct* states: "9.01 Bases for assessments (a) Psychologists base the opinions contained in their recommendations, reports, and diagnostic or evaluative statements, including forensic testimony, on information and techniques sufficient to substantiate their findings."

The APA guideline 9.01 is consistent with Federal Rule 702 "Testimony by Expert Witnesses." It states that,

> (a) The expert's scientific, technical, or other specialized knowledge will help the trier of fact to understand the evidence or to determine a fact in issue; (b) The testimony is based on sufficient facts or data;

(c) The testimony is the product of reliable principles and methods; and (d) The expert has reliably applied the principles and methods to the facts of the case.

This Visser, Book, and Volk study is based on validated expert rating scales on Mental Functioning that is in keeping with all mental health professional ethics codes and legal standards.

Electing well-qualified leaders is essential for the health and welfare of a nation and its citizens. Although most people will vote according to their personality, party loyalty and hot-button issues, there are many voters who will consider information about a candidate's character and temperament (Visser, Book, & Volk, 2017). In Visser, Book, and Volk's 2018 article "Measuring the Next President's Personality Using an Expert Raters Method," they reported, "The online academic influence measuring tool, Altmetrics, noted that our article was in the top 2 percent of all research articles tracked (over 7.2 million of them) with regard to the amount of media attention it received" (p. 8). Since presidential elections are often very close, this information is clearly valued and could make a significant difference.

It Is important to consider a candidate's capacity for mature leadership by assessing the more nuanced and detailed Mental Functioning items that are assessed: weight of evidence, insightfulness, communication skills, making rational and realistic decisions, high stress tolerance, resiliency and adaptation, good impulse control, and healthy standards and ideals. The PDC-2's Mental Functioning scale showed a high degree of utility for measuring these traits and was useful for informing the voting public.

This study demonstrated that the PDC-2's Mental Functioning scale was sensitive to both large and subtle differences in political leaders (with scores ranging from: 1 = Severe Defects, to 5 = Healthy). The Mental Functioning scale measured Volodymyr Zelensky with an average score of 4.57 out of a possible 5 with an overall percentage of 91 percent. This score indicates a psychologically healthy leader.

Vladimir Putin's average Mental Functioning score was only 2.04, or an overall percentage of 41 percent, which is in the severe mental illness range.

Donald Trump was consistently rated lower than Putin with an average Mental Functioning score of only 1.25, or just 25 percent level of Mental Functioning or in the severe mental illness range. Putin and Trump both scored in the dangerous range in all 12 Mental Functions.

Both Putin and Trump:

1 Have a poor capacity for regulation, attention, and learning that includes the capacity to attend to and process information, focus, and learn from experience.
2 Have a poor capacity for affective range, communication, and understanding.

3 Have a poor capacity for mentalization and reflective functioning that includes the capacity to understand and interpret the behavior of self and others in terms of mental states (e.g., needs, desires, feelings, beliefs, goals, intentions, and motivations), and ability to take another person's perspective.
4 Have a poor capacity to distinguish self from other, fantasy from reality, internal representations from external objects and present from past and future and to construct and maintain a differentiated, realistic, coherent, complex representation of self (identity).
5 Have a poor capacity for relationships and intimacy.
6 Have a poor capacity for self-esteem regulation being neither unrealistically high nor unrealistically low.
7 Have a poor capacity for impulse control and regulation.
8 Have a poor capacity for defensive functioning that includes the capacity to modulate anxiety, or threat to self-esteem without excessive distortion in self-perception and reality testing, and without making excessive use of denial, projection, splitting, idealization/devaluation, or acting out.
9 Have a poor capacity for adaptation, resiliency, and strength including the capacity to adjust to unexpected events and changing circumstances, and the ability to cope effectively and creatively when confronted with uncertainty, loss, stress, and challenge.
10 Have poor self-observing capacities (psychological mindedness), including the individual's ability to observe his or her own internal life mindfully and realistically and use this information adaptively to facilitate self-awareness.
11 Have a poor capacity to construct and use internal standards and ideals, including the capacity to formulate values, standards and ideals and the ability to make mindful decisions based on a set of coherent, flexible, and internally consistent underlying moral principles.
12 Have a poor capacity for meaning and purpose, including the capacity for directedness and purpose, a concern for succeeding generations, and a spirituality (not necessarily expressed as traditional religiosity) that imbues one's life with meaning.

Putin was able to actualize his destructiveness as a dictator of Russia, while Trump was held in check by a liberal democracy's free press, rule of law and free elections.

We estimate that candidates with percentage scores less than 70 are not fit to serve for high office. The expert ratings of the levels of mental functioning of Putin and Trump clearly indicate their potential for dangerous and destructive leadership.

We hope the Mental Functioning level (20–100 percent), and the standard of at least a level of 70 percent will be easily understood by the public and prove useful in informing voters in the future.

History informs us that the malignant mental illness of autocratic leaders causes the worst avoidable suffering. It is the duty of experts to educate and warn of such dangers.

References

American Psychological Association (2016) *Ethical Principles of Psychologists and Code of Conduct.* www.apa.org/ethics/code/ethics-code-2017.pdf

Ashton, M.C., & Lee, K. (2007). Empirical, theoretical, and practical advantages of the HEXACO model of personality structure. *Personality and Social Psychology Review,* 11(2), 150–166.

Baker, P. & Glasser, S. (2022). *The Divider: Trump in the White House, 2017–2021.* Doubleday.

Bartels, M., van Weegen, F.I., van Beijsterveldt, C.E., Carlier, M., Polderman, T.J., Hoekstra, R.A. & Boomsma, D.I. (2012). The five factor model of personality and intelligence: A twin study on the relationship between the two constructs. *Personality and Individual Differences,* 53(4), 368–373.

Bender, M. C. (2021). *Frankly, we did win this election: The inside story of how Trump lost.* Twelve.

Bodholdt, R.H. (2000). Assessing psychopathy: Interpersonal aspects and clinical interviewing. *The clinical and forensic assessment of psychopathy: A practitioner's guide.* Routledge, p. 203.

Dana, J., Dawes, R., & Peterson, N. (2013). Belief in the unstructured interview: The persistence of an illusion. *Judgment and Decision Making,* 8(5), 512.

Edwards, G.S., & Rushin, S. (2018). The effect of President Trump's election on hate crimes. https://dx.doi.org/10.2139/ssrn.3102652

Feinberg, A., Branton, R., & Martinez-Ebers, V. (2022). The Trump effect: how 2016 campaign rallies explain spikes in hate. *PS: Political Science & Politics,* 55(2), 257–265.

Gordon, R.M. (2010). The Psychodynamic Diagnostic Manual (PDM). In I. Weiner and E. Craighead, (Eds.) *Corsini's Encyclopedia of Psychology* (4th ed., volume 3). John Wiley and Sons, pp. 1312–1315.

Gordon, R.M. (2022). The Psychodynamic Diagnostic Manual-2 for the Assessment of Malignant Narcissistic, Psychopathic, and Sadistic Personality Syndromes: Implications for Criminology and Politics. Ed.David N. Weisstub; International Congress on Law and Mental Health, July, Lyon, France, p. 163. www.researchgate.net/publication/361348253_The_Psychodynamic_Diagnostic_Manual-2_for_the_Assessment_of_Malignant_Narcissistic_Psychopathic_and_Sadistic_Personality_Syndromes_Implications_for_Criminology_and_Politics

Gordon, R.M., & Bornstein, R.F. (2012). A practical tool to integrate and operationalize the PDM with the ICD or DSM. www.mmpi-info.com/pdm-blog

Gordon, R.M. & Bornstein, R.F. (2018). Construct Validity of the Psychodiagnostic Chart: A Transdiagnostic Measure of Personality Organization, Personality Syndromes, Mental Functioning, and Symptomatology. *Psychoanalytic Psychology,* 35(2), 280–288. http://dx.doi.org/10.1037/pap0000142

Gordon, R.M. & Stoffey, R.W. (2014). Operationalizing the Psychodynamic Diagnostic Manual: a Preliminary Study of the Psychodiagnostic Chart (PDC), *Bulletin of the Menninger Clinic*, 78, 1, 1–15.

Greiffenstein, M.F., John Baker, W., Tsushima, W.T., Boone, K., & Fox, D.D. (2010). MMPI-2 validity scores in defense-versus plaintiff-selected examinations: A repeated measures study of examiner effects. *The Clinical Neuropsychologist*, 24(2), 305–314.

Jonason, P.K., & McCain, J. (2012). Using the HEXACO model to test the validity of the Dirty Dozen measure of the Dark Triad. *Personality and Individual Differences*, 53(7), 935–938.

Jones, D.N., & Paulhus, D.L. (2014). Introducing the short dark triad (SD3) a brief measure of dark personality traits. *Assessment*, 21(1), 28–41.

Kowert, P.A. (1996). Where "Does" the Buck Stop?: Assessing the impact of presidential personality. *Political Psychology*, 421–452.

Lee, K., & Ashton, M.C. (2005). Psychopathy, Machiavellianism, and narcissism in the Five-Factor Model and the HEXACO model of personality structure. *Personality and Individual Differences*, 38(7), 1571–1582.

Lee, K., & Ashton, M.C. (2014). The dark triad, the big five, and the HEXACO model. *Personality and Individual Differences*, 67, 2–5.

Lilienfeld, S.O., Miller, J.D., & Lynam, D.R. (2018). The Goldwater Rule: Perspectives from, and implications for, psychological science. *Perspectives on Psychological Science*, 13(1), 3–27.

Lingiardi, V., & McWilliams, N. (Eds.). (2017). *Psychodynamic diagnostic manual: PDM-2*. Guilford Publications.

McBride, J. (2021). Authoritarianism and Religion: Trump and White Evangelicals in Cultural Perspective. *The GCAS Review Journal*, 1, 1,1.

Messina, K.E. (2022). *Resurgence of Global Populism: A Psychoanalytic Study of Projective Identification, Blame-Shifting and the Corruption of Democracy*. Taylor & Francis.

Meyer, G.J., Finn, S.E., Eyde, L.D., Kay, G.G., Moreland, K.L., Dies, R.R., ... & Reed, G.M. (2001). Psychological testing and psychological assessment: A review of evidence and issues. *American Psychologist*, 56(2), 128.

McCrae, R.R., & Costa, P.T. (1985). The NEO personality inventory manual. *Psychological Assessment Resources*, Odessa.

McDermott, R. (2020). Leadership and the strategic emotional manipulation of political identity: An evolutionary perspective. *The Leadership Quarterly*, 31(2), 101275.

Murray, R.K., & Blessing, T.H. (2010). *Greatness in the White House: Rating the Presidents, from Washington Through Ronald Reagan* (Vol. 50). Penn State Press.

Nai, A., & Toros, E. (2020). The peculiar personality of strongmen: comparing the Big Five and Dark Triad traits of autocrats and non-autocrats. *Political Research Exchange*, 2(1), 1707697.

Rice, M.G., Remmel, M.L., & Mondak, J.J. (2021). Personality on the hill: Expert evaluations of US senators' psychological traits. *Political Research Quarterly*, 74(3), 674–687.

Rubenzer, S.J., & Faschingbauer, T.R. (2004). *Personality, character, and leadership in the White House: Psychologists assess the presidents*. Potomac Books, Inc.

Simonton, D.K. (2002). Intelligence and presidential greatness: Equation replication using updated IQ estimates.

Visser, B.A., Book, A.S., & Volk, A.A. (2017). Is Hillary dishonest and Donald narcissistic? A HEXACO analysis of the presidential candidates' public personas. *Personality and Individual Differences*, 106, 281–286.

Visser, B.A., Book, A., & Volk, A. (2018). *Measuring the Next President's Personality Using an Expert Raters Method*. SAGE Publications Ltd.

Woodward, B., & Costa, R. (2021). *Peril*. Simon & Schuster.

Xu, X., & Plaks, J.E. (2022). Aspect-level personality characteristics of US Presidential candidate supporters in the 2016 and 2020 elections. *Social Psychological and Personality Science*, 19485506221113954.

PART 5

A Scholar Looks at Vladimir Putin through the Lens of Russian Literature

Chapter 7

Dear Vladimir Putin

If You've Read Dostoyevsky, You've Tragically Misunderstood Him—Austin Ratner on Russian Imperialism and Misreading *The Brothers Karamazov*

Austin Ratner

In retrospect, the opening ceremonies of the 2014 Winter Olympics in Sochi, Russia, foreshadowed what Putin has done in recent years like a scene from a Russian novel. That night of February 7, 2014, before billions of viewers, Vladimir Putin pursued a foolhardy, tragic agenda: to school the world in Russian greatness. His means would be a dazzling, animated history lesson, formatted like a children's alphabet book. Famous Russians each got their own letter.

"D" was for Dostoyevsky. "T" was for Tolstoy. No one understood at the time that a shot had been fired; mere days after the 2014 Winter Games ended, Putin would flex Russian power for real by invading Crimea. The great Russian authors onscreen that night had been conscripted to the cause of "империя"—"empire"—without their knowledge or consent.

They could not consent because they were, conveniently, dead. Were he alive, Tolstoy could not have endorsed Putin's aggression. After documenting the horrors of the original Crimean War in his *Sevastopol Sketches*, Tolstoy became a pacifist. But what about Dostoyevsky, who was supposedly a pan-Slavic nationalist? Some speculate that the author of *Crime and Punishment* and *The Brothers Karamazov* would have cheered Putin on. Others plead, "Don't blame Dostoyevsky."

Putin surely didn't care one way or the other, so long as the message of Russian might was made clear. The message that February evening, however, came with a literal asterisk. When the alphabet of Russian greatness was complete, five glowing animatronic snowflakes slowly opened into the interlocking Olympic rings. Except the one in the upper right corner didn't open. It just stayed a snowflake, like an asterisk denoting something awry. There's undoubtedly someone in Siberia right now wishing that snowflake had done its job.

Dostoyevsky, who himself served time in Siberia for offending the czar and was only spared execution at the last possible second, probably would have avoided crossing Putin in public. But his artwork speaks for itself. His character Fetyukovich, a defense attorney in *The Brothers Karamazov*, said it straight out: "[F]orward, Russia, and intimidate, intimidate us not with your furied *troikas*, from which all nations stand aside in sickened loathing!"[1] As if to eliminate any ambiguity about Dostoyevsky's attitude to Russian national power, he has the prosecutor in the same trial say much the same thing with the same imagery:

> [O]ur fateful *troika* is rushing headlong, and possibly to its doom ... And if for the present the other nations still stand back from the headlong-galloping *troika*, then it is perhaps not at all out of deference to it, as the poet would like, but simply out of horror ... Out of horror, and possibly out of loathing.

Dostoyevsky may or may not have embraced Russian chauvinism, but if he did, he is certainly not beloved around the globe for *that*. He is internationally beloved for his empathic and humanistic artwork. The central meanings and achievements of Dostoevsky's masterpiece *The Brothers Karamazov*, which Sigmund Freud in 1928 called "the most magnificent novel ever written," in fact undercut everything Putin stands for.

"Out of the crooked timber of humanity, no straight thing was ever made," Immanuel Kant famously wrote in 1784. Fyodor Dostoyevsky's *The Brothers Karamazov* is like a botanist's illustration of that crooked timber. Within this behemoth novel's pages you encounter a giant, thorny bramble of feelings like a prickly Russian thistle, rendered minutely and comprehensively down to every last twisted, tangled stem and thorn. Pan-Slavic nationalist, existentialist, or Russian Orthodox monk—no, none of these labels does justice to the tortured epileptic visionary Dostoyevsky. He was first and foremost a portraitist of the crooked timber of the soul, the great psychoanalyst among creative writers. His specialty was observing and depicting feelings and their slippery relationship with consciousness.

Like Shakespeare before him and Freud after him, Dostoyevsky recognized that feelings can unconsciously distort conscious thinking. Repeatedly, his characters' painful feelings wriggle out from under contemplation, often by means of "motivated forgetting," as experimental psychologist Lester Luborsky called such momentary instances of repression. For example, when the central character Dmitry (aka Mitya) Karamazov shows up at his beloved Grushenka's house and Fenya the maid asks him why he's covered in blood, he immediately forgets her question: "What hands you have, Dmitry Fyodorovich, all covered in blood!"

"Yes," Mitya replied in mechanical fashion, took an absentminded glance at his hands and at once forgot about them and about Fenya's question." We all experience this sort of "motivated forgetting," even under less fraught circumstances. It happens, for example, when we *forget* to do something we *don't want* to do. I don't have any hard data, but I'm pretty sure people forget to go to the dentist more than they forget to go to the movies.

Like Shakespeare before him and Freud after him, Dostoyevsky recognized that feelings can unconsciously distort conscious thinking. Clifton Fadiman consequently called Dostoyevsky "the dramatist of the unconscious and what is called the abnormal." Having peeked behind the curtain at feelings denied or repressed, Dostoyevsky further recognized that "abnormal" feelings are actually ... normal. "Abnormal" is just a name that conscience applies to certain antisocial feelings to bar them from the proscenium of consciousness and hide them backstage, as it were, behind the stage curtains.

Dostoyevsky goes just as far as Freud in owning up to "abnormal" feelings and arrives at a similar destination—that weird and icky constellation of childhood feelings Freud labeled the "Oedipus Complex." His main character Mitya, who's abandoned by his mother and forgotten by his father, hates his father so much that he threatens to kill him. He feels the absence of a mother's love so acutely that he becomes entangled in competition with his father for the love of the same woman, the dominatrix Grushenka.

Dostoyevsky uses the art of realist fiction to put us directly in Mitya's shoes in a way neither Shakespeare nor Freud ever could. At Mitya's trial for patricide, Dr. Herzenstube recalls the accused's childhood like this:

> And yet he was a youth of sensitivity and gratitude, oh, I remember him very well when he was an urchin so high, left in the backyard of his father's house, running around without any boots on and with his little trousers held up by a single button ...

We *experience* Mitya's neglect in this scene and *feel* his loathing for his father, and his need for a mother's love and protection.

If some readers empathize with the child, but not with the adult man's rage and needs, Dostoyevsky seems to plead with them that they should. He makes the confession of "abnormal," antisocial feelings into a virtue in *The Brothers Karamazov*. Admitting and verbalizing such feelings helps brothers Ivan and Mitya Karamazov *not* act on them. They "speak daggers," as Hamlet says, "but use none."

Dostoyevsky may or may not have embraced Russian chauvinism, but if he did, he is certainly not beloved around the globe for *that*.

Ivan, for instance, stresses his right to murderous wishes, even the wish to kill his own father. "Be assured that I shall always defend him [their father, Fyodor]," Ivan says to younger brother Alyosha. "But where my desires are concerned, in the given instance I leave myself ample latitude." Mitya makes the same distinction between feeling and doing when he confesses to the police investigating his father's murder: "I did not kill him. But I wanted to!"

When we don't know what we feel or deny what we feel because it's too shameful or guilt-provoking, we deprive ourselves of the chance to filter our feelings through the conscious and rational decision-making processes of the cerebral frontal lobe. When feeling bypasses awareness, it can distort thought and lead straight to impetuous action.

Ah, Putin! You say you read *The Brothers Karamazov*, but if only you had understood it! If only you'd been able to admit to the feelings in your heart—your insane, jealous hatred of "the West," a monolith looming above in your imagination—you might have spared yourself, your people, and Ukraine this catastrophe.

But you don't understand what makes Russia's great writers great, nor are you brave enough to look within as they do. When that snowflake didn't open, the world heard your ego cracking like Siberian ice with humiliation and fury.

Dostoyevsky might have had more sympathy for that broken snowflake, for the imperfection and vulnerability it signified—even for the humiliation and fury it provoked. He had the conviction that in the realm of feeling, abnormal is normal—the conviction that vulnerability, while hard to feel, must be felt. His son Alyosha died just before he turned 3 years old, like a snowflake that did not open. Dostoyevsky began work on *The Brothers Karamazov* right after this devastating event and named the saintly Alyosha Karamazov after his son.

Nietzsche argued that

> the strength of a spirit should be measured according to how much of the "truth" one could still barely endure—or to put it more clearly, to what degree one would *require* it to be thinned down, shrouded, sweetened, blunted, falsified.

Those who have read and understood *The Brothers Karamazov* know exactly how to measure Dostoyevsky—and how to measure Putin.

Note

1 The *troika* is a three-horse sleigh that has long been a national symbol in Russia. The specific image of other nations yielding to the *troika* of the Russian state originates with Nikolai Gogol's *Dead Souls*. Notwithstanding the possible nationalist overtones of the famous *troika* passage, *Dead Souls* satirizes Russia's shortcomings more than it celebrates Russian greatness. When Gogol shared the manuscript of the novella with Pushkin, it actually caused Pushkin to remark, "God! What a sad country Russia is!"

Conclusion

Since this book does not purport to report news and is based on the opinions of its editor and contributors, every attempt has been made to welcome different points of view from professionals with expertise in psychoanalysis, psychiatry, trauma, international conflict resolution, European and Russia history, Russian literature, psychohistory, and quantitative research. With this orientation in mind, each contributor has brought something unique to the table.

That being said, writing a conclusion about an ongoing conflict is challenging because of the fluid nature of war as well as the fact that people around the world receive biased news. In the best-case scenario, this is due to the fact that most news reports read in print, seen on television or learned through social media contain some facts as well as the reporter's or newscaster's perspective; there is often no way to eliminate that bias. When nefarious characters wish to deceive people, fake news and false information are purposely distributed with erroneous facts to obtain power, create chaos, or for a number of other reasons that are disruptive. If we were able to learn factual information that was not laced with opinion, it would be the most optimal way to relay the news so people could decide for themselves what they believe about any given situation.

As a way to provide at least nuggets of hope for the future, Messina asks that we consider the importance of pivoting toward evidence and truth-telling, since we can only reestablish trust if we believe in the information we hear.

The Influence from the West

With regard to the invasion of Ukraine, in spite of the horrendous state of affairs for the people who live in this war-torn country, Gill and Messina, like Sachs and Mearsheimer, believe Putin was provoked into starting the war because of many broken promises the West made to Gorbachev about NATO's plans for the future. From 1989 to 1991 many Western leaders continued to reassure Russia that additional countries would not be added to the Alliance. James Baker, the Secretary of State under George H.W. Bush made the now infamous "not an inch" statement on at least three occasions. The crucial passage is this:

> if the United States keeps its presence in Germany within the framework of NATO, not an inch of NATO's present military jurisdiction will spread in an eastern direction.
> (Document 6, National Security Archive, 1990)

Other leaders from European countries supported the statement that was made by Baker and reiterated by Bush. Such luminaries as Genscher, Kohl, Gates, Mitterrand, Thatcher, Hurd, Major, and Woerner were also "looking to reassure the Soviets" of that pledge, according to classified documents from the National Security Archive (Puryear, 2022).

The promises Baker and Bush made to Gorbachev don't justify the war by any means, but Putin, as well as his predecessors, have warned the West on numerous occasions to stop the expansion of NATO. This has been common knowledge among US officials since George H. W. Bush left office.

Experts warned the West that trouble of "epic proportions" would follow any NATO expansion, and tragedy—a "violent breach"—was precisely the result. As analysts foresaw: "We are now paying the price for US foreign policy establishment's myopia and arrogance" (Carpenter, 2022).

For Petschauer, the cause of the war is not simple. It encompasses a broad array of psychological, cultural, and historical factors that he sees as making their own unique contribution to Putin's behavior. Petschauer also poses important questions. Why did Putin do it? Why did he order the attack? Why did he want to invade a sovereign country? In answering his questions, he says Putin initiated the war because he is an authoritarian leader and that's what such leaders do; authoritarian leaders start wars.

Types of Assessments used to Evaluate Putin: Quantitative and Psychobiography

Messina agrees that it is optimal to develop some type of assessment tool to evaluate potential candidates who wish to hold top-level positions, such as people who want to make a bid for the White House. It is her hope that those who step up and announce their wish to lead our country will be among a group who value truth for the good of the country and not put their own wish for self-aggrandizement, attained by telling lies, ahead of what is important for the people they want to lead.

Developmental Psychobiography

Volkan and Javakhishvili think it is difficult to assess a world leader from a distance and proceeded cautiously with their assessment of Putin because they have never met Putin, nor do they know anyone who personally knows him. However, they also believe if enough accurate information is available about a person's life, it is possible to learn a great about him or her by constructing a thorough developmental psychobiography. Their technique, which was developed over a number of years by many experts in child, adolescent, and adult development, including Volkan and several colleagues, covers internal conscious and unconscious fantasies and external aspects of development from infancy through late adulthood.

Extrapolating through Russian Literature

Ratner, in his beautifully written piece about Putin's misunderstanding of *The Brothers Karamazov*, doesn't suffer fools gladly. He makes it perfectly clear that Putin doesn't comprehend the profound message of one of the greatest writers in modern history; Sigmund Freud said, in 1928, he thought *The Brothers Karamazov* was "the most magnificent novel ever written."

Dostoyevsky devoted a good deal of time thinking about the importance of free will as well as about the consequences one must face based on the choices he or she makes. Putin doesn't appear to be thinking about the significance of these concepts, in spite of his love of Dostoyevsky's work. Is it because he doesn't understand what his ideas mean, or because he knows the meaning but doesn't care? Messina agrees with Ratner but suspects Putin's capacity to understand the meaning of free will is limited because he has never experienced living in an environment where this idea was valued.

Putin as a Replacement Child and His Exposure to Trauma

Javakhishvili and Volkan stress the importance of the replacement child theory in trying to explain Putin's psycho-political mode, believing that Putin falls within their definition: "it is highly likely he held this position for his mother because she lost two children before he was born." In such cases "the mother who has an image of the dead child, treats the second one [or in this case the third child] as the reservoir where the dead child can be kept 'alive.'" (Volkan and Jana, 2022, p. 143).

They also talk about Bion's alpha function, which occurs when an available mother mentally "takes in a child's intense anxiety" and transforms it into something that is more palatable; a level of tension he or she can tolerate. In Putin's case it is unlikely that this happened.

The extreme hardships that young Putin experienced, both physical and emotional, in the end outweighed any lasting help his parents were able to provide.

> Living in a rat-infested building with parents who were too traumatized to give a young boy the love and care he needed might have created a chaotic state of mind. He was burdened with their wartime trauma. With no family … where was the love, kindness, and affection that children must have in order to prosper?
>
> (Volkan and Jana, 2022, p. 65)

Petschauer also believes the misery that Putin's parents endured during the Siege of Leningrad traumatized them as well as their son Vladimir. Although he wasn't born until after the Siege ended, intergenerational trauma continues for years if it is not worked through. Messina agrees that Putin suffered from the Siege, albeit indirectly.

Petschauer considered a variety of potential causative factors that might have contributed to the formation of Putin's personality. They include Russian fear of encirclement, occasioned by World War I and World War II and Napoleon's invasion in the early 19th century which was amplified by "restraining and holding abuses in childhood" reflective of common Russian childcare practice. He also believes that being born into a traumatized family increases the likelihood that one can turn to violence as a means of addressing the pain of transgenerational trauma. A possible identification with heroic, larger-than-life Russian figures such as Peter the Great may have facilitated a sense of being powerful, superior, and chosen. His sense of inferiority could also have led Putin to project what he can't tolerate about himself onto others.

Messina agrees that the concept of intergenerational or transgenerational trauma acknowledges that exposure to extremely adverse events affects individuals to such a great extent that their offspring find themselves grappling with their parents' post-traumatic state. She also believes Putin's childhood appeared to have been horrendous and opens a window into how and why events in Leningrad, Chechnya and Ukraine are uncannily similar. As a hypothesis, the plan to return Chechnya to Russian control seems to be very similar to a wish Putin may have to reunite Ukraine with Russia.

Based on his traumatic childhood and the deprivation he endured, Putin seems to be repeating a form of his earlier experiences which some mental health experts call a *traumatic reenactment*. This is a new term for Freud's *repetition compulsion* which involves repeating painful physical and emotional experiences of the past again and again. When trauma is not worked through, events of the past are repeated (Freud, 1914, p. 145–156). Amplifying this phenomenon is a second consideration: a "forgotten" experience from early childhood may reemerge later in life as not just a memory but an act; such an act may be violent or uncontrolled (Freud, 1914).

Freud's idea is a complex concept since much of what is experienced when one goes through traumatic events in life is repressed or suppressed. It can be assumed that Freud's concept of the repetition compulsion comes into play with a person like Putin since the trauma he and his parents experienced presumably wasn't worked through. The only other possibility from this vantage point is that some aspect of what was experienced is repeated.

References

Carpenter, T. (2022, February 28). Many predicted NATO expansion would lead to war. Those warnings were ignored. *The Guardian*. www.theguardian.com/commentisfree/2022/feb/28/nato-expansion-war-russia-ukraine

Freud, S. (1914). 12. *The Standard Edition of the Complete Psychological Works of Sigmund Freud* (pp. 145–156). Standard Edition. https://marcuse.faculty.history.ucsb.edu/classes/201/articles/1914FreudRemembering.pdf

National Security Archive. (1990, February 1). *NATO expansion: What Gorbachev heard*. National Security Archive. https://nsarchive.gwu.edu/briefing-book/russia-programs/2017-12-12/nato-expansion-what-gorbachev-heard-western-leaders-early

Puryear, E. (2022, May 3). Blame NATO for the Ukrainian War. www.blackagendareport.com/blame-nato-ukraine-war

Streeck, W. (2023, May 1). A bipolar order. *New Left Review*. https://newleftreview.org/sidecar/posts/a-bipolar-order

Volkan, V., & Javakhishvili, J.D. (2022). Invasion of Ukraine: Observations on leader-followers relationships. *The American Journal of Psychoanalysis, 82*(2), 189–209. https://doi.org/10.1057/s11231-022-09349-8

Epilogue

The editor and contributors to this book have presented different views of Vladimir Putin and the war in Ukraine. Some think his invasion was unprovoked, while other authors see it differently.

When all is said and done, we do not *know* why Putin invaded Ukraine, but we all believe what he has done is devastating to the Ukrainian people.

It is my hope as editor of this book that the insights we have provided will help readers continue to think about the ever-evolving situation in Ukraine and decide for themselves what they believe is true.

With regard to the future, the Ukrainian War could last a long time if a course correction is not made. Taking responsibility for how various parties got involved in the conflict could make a major difference when thinking about and preparing for ending the war.

As in any dispute, whether it is between two people, between large groups, or among countries, it is imperative to consider what the other side believes to be the cause of the altercation, skirmish, or full-blown combat. This does not imply agreement or justification, but a recognition that there are many reasons that motivate human behavior.

As we move forward, one thing is imperative: the major leaders involved in this war must begin to talk to each other directly or through mediators if direct communication is not possible. Perhaps they might give thought to a lesson from history by considering the frequency of communication between John F. Kennedy and Nikita Khrushchev during the Cuban Missile Crisis: These men communicated virtually every day (Kennedy, & Khruschev, 1962). Although the editor and contributors have different ideas about why the war in Ukraine began, they have worked together in an atmosphere of respect. It is their hope that this model can be used in other situations where groups become too polarized to work out their differences.

One reason this is so difficult was said well by a reporter from *The Guardian* who recently wrote an opinion piece which summarizes much of what we are facing in a world where many disparate agendas bombard the internet as well as person-to-person exchanges of information. That writer alluded to the Italian perspective about politics called *dietrismo*, or a "habitualized conviction that what you see is designed to hide what you get, by powers operating behind"—*dietro*—"a curtain that divides the world into a stage and a backstage." The action takes place upon the backstage, while the "stage" itself incorporates a degree of misrepresentation.

See, for example, the possibly manufactured story of the Nord Stream pipeline explosions. Passing from the August *New York Times* on to the German weekly *Die Zeit*, the story may have been "concocted" for purposes of disinformation or providing a false trail for other media and the public to follow.

Is this the world we want to live in? Is it a place we want our children to inherit? Is it possible to slow down the rapid expansion of *dietrismo*? Is peace possible? Could we learn from Desmond Tutu, Nelson Mandela, and their Truth and Reconciliation plan? Is there a way to find peace in Ukraine? While the answers to these questions are not known, pivoting toward evidence in order to find the truth, which builds trust, could help us back out of the rabbit hole we are in that is filled with lies, dishonesty, false information and fake news.

Reference

Kennedy, J., & Khruschev, N. (1962). Kennedy–Khruschev correspondence during the Cuban Missile Crisis (October 1962–December 1962). *Foreign Relations of the United States, 1961–1963, Volume VI, Kennedy-Khrushchev Exchanges*. Department of State. www.jfklibrary.org/learn/about-jfk/life-of-john-f-kennedy/fast-facts-john-f-kennedy/kennedy-khrushchev-correspondence-during-cuban-missile-crisis.

Editor and Contributors

Karyne E. Messina, Ed.D., earned master's and doctoral degrees from the George Washington University. She is a licensed psychologist and psychoanalyst and is on the medical staff of Suburban Hospital in Bethesda, Maryland, which is part of Johns Hopkins Medicine. She is a Training and Supervision Analyst at the Washington Baltimore Center for Psychoanalysis. Her books include *Misogyny, Projective Identification and Mentalization, Psychoanalytic, Social and Institutional Manifestations; Aftermath: Healing from the Trump Presidency*; and *Resurgence of Global Populism: A Psychoanalytic Study of Blame-Shifting and the Corruption of Democracy*. She is currently editing a book on the importance of truth and the need for evidence.

Harry Gill, M.D., earned a medical degree from the University of Zagreb School of Medicine in Croatia. He holds a Ph.D. in neuroscience and psychology from Iowa State University. He is currently the president of HGMD, LLC, a private practice offering psychoanalytic psychotherapy and medication management in New York City and Chevy Chase, Maryland. In addition, he serves as an assistant clinical professor in Psychiatry and Behavioral Sciences at the George Washington University and as the medical director for Embark in Cabin John, Maryland, and J Snyder Therapeutic Services in Blue Bell, Pennsylvania. Dr. Gill is board-certified by the American Board of Psychiatry and Neurology.

Robert M. Gordon, Ph.D., ABPP, is a licensed psychologist, diplomate of clinical psychology, a diplomate of psychoanalysis, and served on the governing council of the American Psychological Association. He was president of the Pennsylvania Psychological Association and received its Distinguished Service Award. He was elected honorary member of the American Psychoanalytic Association. He authored many scholarly articles and books in the areas of ethics, the MMPI-2, psychotherapy, relationships, forensic psychology, personality assessment, diagnoses, the

Psychodynamic Diagnostic Manual, a PDM-2 editor and researcher, and co-author of the Psychodiagnostic Chart. Dr. Gordon is rated by ResearchGate as a top researcher. He has an international consulting practice.

Jana D. Javakhishvili, Ph.D., is a professor of psychology at Ilia State University, Tbilisi, Georgia. She is Past President of the European Society for Traumatic Stress Studies. Currently, she is on the board of directors of the International Society for Traumatic Stress Studies, and trustee of the Dart Center for Journalism and Trauma Europe. She serves on the editorial board of the European Journal of Psychotraumatology. She is heavily engaged in the projects of the Federation Global Initiative on Psychiatry focused on improving human rights-based mental health care in Georgia, Kyrgyzstan, Sri Lanka, Ukraine, and other war and political oppression-affected countries.

Peter W. Petschauer has a Ph.D. from New York University, and taught at Appalachian State University (ASU) from 1968 to 2006, initially offering courses in European and Russian history, and later concerning women and children. He served on two arts-related boards at ASU and on two boards of psycho-historical journals. His books include *Was man so Alles lernt*; *In Troubled Times Beauty* (poetry); *Listen to Rarely Heard Voices*; *An Immigrant in the 1960s. Finding Hope and Success in New York City*; *Hopes and Fears. Past and Present* (poetry); *A Perfect Portrait*, about a young female artist in 18th-century Weimar; *In the Face of Evil. The Sustenance of Traditions*; *The Father and the SS*. He has written 200 articles in journals and collections, and presented several hundred lectures.

Austin Ratner, M.D., is author of four books, including the Rohr-Prize-winning novel *The Jump Artist*, called "brilliant" by *The Guardian* and "remarkable" by *Harper's Magazine*. He also wrote *The Psychoanalyst's Aversion to Proof* which Mark Solms has said "could help determine the future direction of American psychiatry and mental science." His essays on literature, psychoanalysis, and politics have appeared in *The New York Times Magazine*, *The Wall Street Journal*, *The Millions*, *The Forward*, and many other publications. He has recently accepted a position as editor of *The American Psychoanalyst* magazine. Visit his website at www.austinratner.com and follow him on Twitter @austinratner.

Vamık Volkan, M.D., is a professor emeritus of psychiatry at the University of Virginia; training and supervising analyst emeritus at the Washington Baltimore Center for Psychoanalysis; president emeritus of the

International Dialogue Initiative and past president of the Virginia Psychoanalytic Society, Turkish-American Neuropsychiatric Society, International Society of Political Psychology, and American College of Psychoanalysts. Dr. Volkan is internationally known for his 40 years of work bringing together conflictual ethnic or national groups for dialogue and mutual understanding. Among his many other honors, he is the founder and president emeritus of the International Dialogue Initiative. A year after his 2002 retirement, he became the Senior Erik Erikson Scholar at the Erikson Institute of the Austen Riggs Center, Stockbridge, Massachusetts for ten years.

Index

Note: **Bold** numbers indicate tables and *italicized* numbers indicate figures.

Abkhazia 92
"abnormal," 125
Abu Ghraib 17–18, 25
Adriatic coast 68
Afghanistan 54, 62
Aftermath, Healing for the Trump Presidency (Messina) 11
aggression, in childhood development 34, 55n2
"agitated" internal world 43, 84
Alexander I 78
Alexander III 91
Alperovitz, Gar 16
alpha function 34, 129
American Faith Angle Forum 40
American Psychoanalytic Association 109
American Psychological Association 115
Andropov, Yuri 41
Anna Freud Center (London) 21
Appalachian State University 78–79
Argumenti i Fakti (*Arguments and Facts*) newspaper 91
Arieli, Yehoshua 83
artists, psychoanalytic writings on 84, 88–89
Atatürk, Kemal 89
attachment 22, 34
Australian Asian Leadership Institute 21
Austro-Hungarian Empire 66
autocratic leaders: Dark Triad traits 106–107; mental illness of 103; safeguards needed 106; wars started by 81, 128
Azov Battalion 70

Baker, James 44; "not one inch" promise 46, 54, 128
Balkan region, geopolitics of 44; and cultural values 63; meddling, justification of 61–62; noncontiguous territories 67, 71; Orthodox Church 65–68
Balkans, war in 61
Bartholomew of Constantinople 66
Beauchamp, Z. 39
beliefs, *versus* known information 29, 31, 45, 52–53
Ben-Gurion, David 83
Berezhkov, Valentin 94
Berlin Wall, fall of 62
Biden, Hunter 13
Biden, Joseph 10–12, 19, 104
Biden administration, and Nord Stream Pipeline 46–47
Bion, Wilfred 34, 55n2, 129
black-and-white thinking 30, 44
Black Sea 61, 67
blame-shifting 2, 10, 30–32
Bolsheviks 91, 93
borders, psychological and physical 34, 97
Borstein, Robert F. 108
Bosnia 67, 68; Neum (city) 67, 71
British National Archive 65
The Brothers Karamazov (Dostoyevsky) 123–126, 129
Burdeau, C. 44–45
Bush, George H.W. 17, 45–46, 127–128
Bush, George H.W. administration 3
Bush, George W. 8–9

Byzantine rulers 77

Calley, William L., Jr. 18
cannibalism, forced on residents of Leningrad 30, 33, 53
Carlson, Tucker 26
Carnegie Endowment for International Peace 52
Carpenter, T. 128
Carter, Jimmy 8
Catherine II 78, 80
certainty, false sense of 53–54
Charles X of Sweden 77–78
Chechnya 36, 52, 80, 92, 130; example of intergenerational trauma 37, *38*
childhood developmental history 1–2, 129; adolescent years 84, 85; aggression in 34; elements of 32, 85; mother-child dyad 34, 55n2, 85; restraining and holding abuses 76, 78, 80, 130. *See also* psychobiography
children: education about World War II 90–91; propaganda directed at 93. *See also* replacement children
Children's Book on War: Diaries 1941–1945 91
China 81; Great Leap Forward policy 104; and Nord Stream Pipeline 47; People's Liberation Army 105
"chosen trauma," 94–95
Chotiner, Isaac 42–43
Clinton, Bill 8, 104
Clinton, Hillary 9–10, 115
Cohen, Josh 70
Cold War 44, 50, 52; Cuban missile crisis 55, 65, 132
Committee to Protect Journalists 105
communication, establishment of 70–71
communication style 2, 11
communism 30, 40, 66
Communist Party of the Soviet Union (CPSU) 93
"compromise formation," 71
Constantinople, Patriarchate of 65
"containment," 34
COVID-19 11, 94
Crimea 42, 54, 80, 81, 93, 123; and Decree No. *117/2021* 65
Crime and Punishment (Dostoyevsky) 123
Crimean War 123
crimes against humanity 97
Croatia 65; and religion 66–67; Roman Catholic Church in 68
Cuban missile crisis 55, 65, 132
cult of personality 42
cultural values 41–42; in Afghanistan 62; complicated relationships with leaders 51–52; laying lives on the line for ideas 41, 61, 66; "Mother Russia," importance of 41, 64; pride in Russia 63
czar, Russian for Caesar 77

D12 Inventory for the Dark Triad 106–108
Daily Beast 47
The Dangerous Case of Donald Trump (Lee) 104
Davis, Eric M. 24
Dead Souls (Gogol) 126n1
death: childhood experiences with 88–89; in children's plays 91; disinterment and chosen trauma 94–95; necrophilia, normalization of 91–92
Decree No. *117/2021* 65
defense mechanisms 11–12, 84; denial 19; importance of 30–32; Russian 76. *See also* blame-shifting; projective identification; splitting
dehumanization 34, 95
democracy 90; effect of lying on 22–23; investigations as part of 25
denial 2, 19
Deriglazova, Larisa 63
Detroit Free Press 14
dictators, as victims of cruelty 35, 37
dietrismo (misrepresentation) 132–133
Die Zeit 133
digital sources of information 22
"Divide et Impera" (Divide and rule) principle 10, 90
Dominion Voting Systems 23–24, 25
Donbas, invasion of 67, 93
Donetsk region 69, 93
Dostoyevsky, Fyodor 123–126, 129
Duma 80–81
"duty to inform," 115

Eastern Europe 79
Eastern European immigrants 36
Eckert, J. 23
ego 12, 33, 84, 88

"ego and superego workings," 71
Elizabeth I of England 77
empathy 24, 71, 104, 124
encirclement, myth of 75, 78, 80.
    See also Leningrad, Siege of
entitlement ideology 96–97
epistemic trust (ET) 21–22
epistemic vigilance 22
Erikson, Erik 84
Estonia 95, 96
Ethical Principles of Psychologists and Code of Conduct (APA) 115
"Eurasianism," 96–97
Europe: peace of broken 75; Peter the Great's exploratory trip to 77.
    See also North Atlantic Treaty Organization, (NATO)
European Council on Foreign Relations 66
European Union 54, 65, 68, 93
Evangelicals, American 108
evidence 1, 53–54, 127; Hitchens' razor 23; overwhelmed by myths 16
expert witnesses 115–116

Fadiman, Clifton 125
fascism 103–104
Federal Rule 702 "Testimony by Expert Witnesses," 115–116
Finland 54, 78
First Person: An Astonishingly Frank Self-Portrait by Russia's President (Putin) 32, 35, 86
Five Factor Measures (Big Five, NEO) personality test 104, 106–107
Flynn, Michael 13
followers: personality traits of 104; "strong leader" supported by 63–64; support regardless of personality traits 108
Fonagy, Peter 21
Foreign Affairs 70
forensic psychology 2
forgetting 19–20
forgiveness 19–20
Founding Fathers 19, 23, 25
Fox News defamation suit 23–24, 25–26
Franz Ferdinand, Archduke 61
Fredrick II 78
Freud, Sigmund 124, 125, 129; repetition compulsion concept 2, 36, 130–131
Frost, David 8

Geneva Convention 18
genocide 94, 103
geopolitical dynamics, simplification of 61
Georgia 43, 54, 92
German reunification 44, 46
glasnost (openness) 79
"glass bubble fantasies," 93–94
Gogol, Nikolai 126n1
"Goldwater Rule," 110
"good" and "bad" people 7, 10, 11, 71n1
Gorbachev, Mikhail 1, 3, 44, 45–46, 54, 79, 81, 127–129
Gordon, Robert M. 108
"greatness" rating 107
Grossman, Vasily 78
The Guardian 132–133
Gulf of Tonkin Resolution 16
Gumilyov, Lev Nikolayevich 97

Hahn, Hannah 36
Haiphong, Danny 47
Hart, Gary 13
hate crimes 104–105
Heath, Donald 80
Hersh, Seymour 18, 46–48
HEXACO 107, 115
The Hill 13
Hiroshima and Nagasaki bombing 14–16
Hitchens, Christopher 23
Hitler, Adolf 37, 80, 95, 103–104
Holodomor 92, iii
Homes Islands (Japan) 16
Hovorun, Cyril 40
Humphrey, Hubert H. 12
Hussein, Saddam 62

"id derivative," 71
identity: large-group 93–97; personal 95
"The Ignorance or How We Produce the Evil" (Miller) 34–35
Ikle, Fred Charles 83
Insurrection of January 6, 2021 (United States) 21, 25, 105
intelligence (IQ) 106
intergenerational trauma: example of 37, 38; and Putin 1–2, 32–33, 35–37, 53, 75–76, 130
internally displaced people (IDP) 92, 93
International Criminal Tribunal for the former Yugoslavia 97
international relations, psychodynamics of 84

International Security Assistance Force in Afghanistan (ISAF) 54
"Invasion of Ukraine: Observations on Leader-followers Relationships" (Volkan and Javakhishvili) 31–32
invasions, Putin's involvement in 92–94. *See also* Ukraine, Putin's invasion of
investigative reporting 25; anonymous sources 47–48; criticism of 44–45; labeling of reporters 45, 46, 47
Iran-Contra affair 17
Iraq, and cultural values 62
Iraq war 9
Itzkowitz, N. 89
Ivan III (Ivan the Great) 77
Ivan the Terrible 51, 77, 80

Japan: Hiroshima and Nagasaki bombing 14–16
Jeremić, Vuk 44
Johnson, Lyndon 16–17
Joint Chiefs of Staff 105
journalists, murdered by Putin 105
Judah, Tim 67, 68

Kabaeva, Alina 89
Kagame, Paul 20
Kant, Immanuel 124
Kelly, John 104
Kennedy, John F. 55, 132
Kennedy, Robert F. 12
Khanna, Ro 70
Khrushchev, Nikita 55, 132
Kinnock, Neil 12
Kirill, Patriarch 40–41, 65–66
Kirk, Alexander 80
Klein, Melanie 55n2, 71n1
knowledge acquisition 22–23
known information 29, 31, 45, 52–53, 132
Kohl, Helmut 44, 46
Kosovo 67, 94
Kotkin, Stephen 41–42
Kurczap-Redlich, Krystyna 87
Kyiv, in Russian history 63, 66, 80

large-group identity 93–97; adulthood changes 96; entitlement ideology 96–97; narcissism 96
Laruelle, Marlene 44–45
Lazar, Prince 94–95
leaders: "agitated" decision-makers 43, 84; communication between 132; and cultural values 51–52; disdain or self-loathing in 31; "glass bubble fantasies," 93–94; great figures, identification with 76, 130; higher standards for 19–20, 26n2; maturity of 103; mental capacity evaluations 106; Muscovite rulers 77; personalities of 83–85; populist 31; reparative 34, 89; rescue fantasies of 33–34, 63, 87–90; responsibility to assess moral character of 22–23; Russian elite Westernised 77–78; "strong leader," 63–64; and trust 24; truthfulness as requirement for 21
Lee, Bandy 104
"Left Lens YouTube" show 47
Leningrad: Chechnya's resemblance to 37, *38*; schooling in 35; spirit of resiliency in 33
Leningrad, Siege of 29–30, 32–33, 53, 75–76, 78, 85–86, 130
Levada Center 104
Levine, Timothy 20
Levitan, Yuri 90
Lewinsky, Monica 8
lies 26n1; democracy, effect on 22–23; *dietrismo* 132–133; explored by psychoanalysts 11–12; fake news 22–26, 127, 133; Hiroshima and Nagasaki bombing 14–16; *Maddox* incident 16–17; not wanting to believe 8, 11–13; number told by Trump 11; "pathological liars," 20; reactions of denial to 8, 11–13; told by Biden 12–13; told by Nixon 8. *See also* truth
Li Zuocheng 105
Los Angeles Times 16
Luborsky, Lester 124
Luhansk, invasion of 67, 93

Macron, Emmanuel 77
Maidan Revolution 93
malignant propaganda 34, 90, 94–97; enhancing shared sense of victimization 95; time collapse 90–91, 95
Mandela, Nelson 13, 20, 26, 133
manifest destiny 41–42
Mao Zedong 37, 103, 104
McGovern, Raymond 47
McNamara, Robert 16
Mearsheimer, John 42–43

"Measuring the Next President's Personality Using an Expert Raters Method" (Visser, Book, and Volk) 116
meddling, justification of 61–62
Medvedev, Dmitri 89
Mein Kampf (Hitler) 95
memories: repressed or "forgotten," 2–3, 35–36; transmission of 88
Mental Functioning scales (PDC-2) 103, 110–116, **113**
mentalization 47–48
Merikangas, James 15
military uniforms, worn as clothing 91
Miller, Alice 34–35, 36–37
Miller, C. 70
Milley, Mark 105
Milošević, Mirjana 94–95
Milošević, Slobodan 94–95, 97
Misogyny, Projective Identification and Mentalization: Psychoanalytic. Social, and Institutional Manifestation (Messina) 9
Modi, Narendra 2
moral responsibility 22–23
Morawiecki, Mateusz 67
Moscovia der Hauptstat in Reissen (von Herberstein) 77
Moscow Times 91–92
mother-child dyad 34, 55n2, 85
Murdock, Rupert 24
Muscovite rulers 77, 80
Mussolini, Benito 83
My Lai Massacre 18–19, 25, 47
mythomania 26n1

Napoleon 78, 130
narcissism 89, 93–94; large-group 96
narcissistic injury 63, 64, 68
"National Militia" (Ukraine) 70
National Museum of the US Navy 16
"National Program of the Patriotic Education of Citizens of the Russian Federation," 90
National Security Archive (George Washington University) 1, 3, 45–46, 54, 128
"nations" (ethnic-centered states) 79
NATO–Russia Council 54
Nazism: "delusional" aspect of Putin's propaganda 93; neo-Nazis in Ukraine 69–70; in Putin's childhood 34; Putin's focus on 40, 43–44, 81, 93; Slavs, memories of 70. *See also* Leningrad, Siege of
necrophilia, normalization of 91–92
"negative selection," 42
Nelson, Justin 24
neo-Nazis 69–70
Neum (city) 67, 71
neuroticism 107
news media: biased reporting 127; fake news 22–26, 127, 133; ignorance of influence on Putin 79
The New Statesman 39–40
The New Yorker 41–43, 47
New York Times 12, 40, 47, 133
Nicholas I 81
Nicholas II 81, 91
Nietzsche, Friedrich 125
Nixon, Richard 8
Nixon administration, and My Lai Massacre 18–19
noncontiguous territories 67, 71
Nord Stream Pipeline 46–48, 133
North Atlantic Treaty Organization, (NATO) 3, 41–42, 79; Article 5, 54; broken promises not to expand 3, 44, 45–46, 54, 64–65, 127–128; denial of agreements 64–65; Eastern expansion events 54–55; NATO Summit (2008) 43; Partnership for Peace program 54; as shadow of itself 80
North Ossetian State University (Vladikavkaz) 78–79
"nostalgia," 63

Obama, Barack 9
"Oedipus Complex," 125
Olinick, Stanley 89
Oliver Stone Interviews with Vladimir Putin 47–51
Omar, Ilhan 11
Oppenheimer, Robert J. 15
Orthodox Church 40–41, 65–68, 76, 97; KGB infiltration of 66; and Russkiy Mir Foundation 97; Serbian 68, 94
Ottoman Empire 89

Paleologos, Sophia 77
paranoia 103, 105
"paranoid-schizoid" position 70, 71n1

Paris Agreement 9
Peek Liz 13
People's Liberation Army of China 105
perestroika (restructuring) 79
Perry, Bruce 36
personality disorders 21, 26n1, 112
personality level of organization 109
personality organization 83–85
personality traits of followers 104
Peter, St. 76
Peter I 76, 81
Peter the Great 39–40, 51, 77, 80, 130
Pfiffner, James 22–23
Piskaryovskoye Cemetery (St. Petersburg) 86
Plaks, J. E. 104
Poland 67
Pollock, George 88–89
Pomerantsev, Peter 51–52
Poniewozik, James 47, 51
populist leaders, disdain or self-loathing in 31
Poroshenko, Petro 66
Potsdam Proclamation/Declaration 16
presidents, US 8–14, 106. *See also specific presidents*
Princip, Gavrilo 61
projective identification 2, 10, 19, 30–32, 130
propaganda: "delusional" aspect of 93; Hitler's view of 95; malignant 34, 90, 94–97; and personality traits 104; US 14
protector/"savior," 64, 65, 95
psychoanalysis 84
psychoanalysts, unconscious rescue fantasies of 89
psychobiography 1, 32, 84–85, 128–129. *See also* childhood developmental history
Psychodiagnostic Chart (PDC-2) 103, 108–115; M-Axis of Mental Functions 110–116, **113**
Psychodynamic Diagnostic Manual (PDM-2) 103, 108–109
psychopathy 106, 107
psychosis **113**, 114
Putin (Short) 53–54
Putin, Vladimir Vladimirovich: 2023 speech on Battle of Stalingrad 43–44; adult life 89–90; aggressiveness of 76; autobiography 32, 35, 86; background of 85–87; beliefs about 29, 45; on breakup of Soviet Union 63; burials and graveyards, preoccupation with 86, 90; communism's influence on 30; early contacts with West 77, 81; family history shared by in 2012 86; father of 75–76, 85–87, 91; fear of being "surrounded," 75, 80; February 7, 2014 speech 123; February 24, 2022 speech 43; feeling of being "less than," 76; first wife of 76, 79, 80, 89; history of youthful troublemaking 75, 76; in "Immortal Regiment" march 91; and intergenerational trauma 1–2, 32–33, 35–37, 53, 75–76, 130; invasions, involvement in 92–94; KGB background 2, 41, 89; known information about 29, 31, 45, 52–53; Kosovo and Ukraine comparison 67; Mental Functioning ratings 103, 112–118, **113**; mother of 30, 32–35, 40, 75–76, 85–87, 129; narcissism of 89, 93–94; paranoia of 105; Piskaryovskoye Cemetery visits 86; as pragmatic leader 41; as protector/"savior" of Russia 64, 65, 95; as replacement child 32–35, 87–89, 90, 129; and rescue fantasies 33–34, 63, 90, 94–97; reticence about personal life 2, 29, 53; and Russia's history 75–79; siblings of 32–33, 85, 86, 89; small stature compensated for 76, 81; speculation about 52–53; Stalin, imitation of 93; Stone interviews 47–51; support of the people for 63–64, 67–68; war crimes of 51, 52, 81, 105; and World War II commemorations 86, 91
Putina, Maria Ivanovna 32–33
Putinism 42

quantitative research 1, 103–120, 128; D12 Inventory for the Dark Triad 106–108; Five Factor Measures (Big Five, NEO) personality test 104, 106–107; HEXACO 107, 115; new research on mental functioning scale 109–110; Psychodiagnostic Chart (PDC-2) 103, 108–1115; Psychodynamic Diagnostic Manual (PDM-2) 103, 108–109; "purposive sampling" of mental health experts

114; Revised NEO Personality Inventory (NEO PI-R) 106
Qui, Linda 12

"rational actor" models 83
Reade, Tara 13
Reagan, Ronald 17
religion 40–41; Roman Catholicism 66–67, 68. *See also* Orthodox Church
"Remembering, Repeating and Work-Though" (Freud) 2
Remnick, David 41–42
reparative leaders 34, 89
repetition compulsions 2–3; traumatic reenactment 36, 130
replacement children 32–35, 87–89, 90, 129; ego functions of 88
repressed or "forgotten" memories 2–3, 35–36
repression: "motivated forgetting," 124–125
rescue fantasies 33–34, 63, 87–90, 94–97. *See also* unconscious fantasies
restraining and holding abuses 76, 78, 80, 130
Resurgence of Global Populism: A Psychoanalytic Study of Blame-Shifting and the Corruption of Democracy (Messina) 31
reunification, psychological reasons for 36, 39–40
revenge 34
Revised NEO Personality Inventory (NEO PI-R) 106
Ridenhour, Ronald 18
right-wing groups 61, 69–70
Rolling Stone 47, 51
Roman Catholic Church 66–68, 97
Rome 77
Roosevelt, Franklin 16
Rossyia governmental TV channel 91
Rurik dynasty 80
Rushe, D. 48, 51
Russia: clothing 1940s-style 91; "Eurasianism," 96–97; Kyiv as original capital of 80; Kyiv in history of 63, 66, 80; linked by Putin with his family 90; manifest destiny 41–42; Muscovite rulers 77; people of overlooked by America and the West 51–52; population 62; reunification as Putin's goal 36, 39–40; Russian fear of being trapped 75, 78; "Russkiy Mir" (Russian World) 96–97; traditional cultural values 41–42; *troika* as symbol of 126n1, 145; violence in war 81; "империя"-"empire," 123. *See also* Soviet Union
Russian Empire 39–40
"Russian Gravediggers Defy Coronavirus to Throw Speed-Digging Contest" 91–92
Russian literature 1, 123–126, 129
"Russkiy Mir" (Russian World) 96–97
Russkiy Mir Foundation 97
Rwanda 20–21

Sachs, Jeffery 45
sadism 36
scapegoats 35
Scheer, Robert 48
Scherer. J. 48, 51
Schlitz, C. 37
Scholz, Olaf 75
Second Chechen War 37, *38*
self-representation 88
senators, United States 106
September 11, 2001 9, 54
Serbian Battle of Kosovo 94
Serbian Orthodox Church 94
serial killers 35
Sevastopol 65
Sevastopol Sketches (Tolstoy) 123
Shakespeare, William 124, 125
Shear, Michael 12
Sherwin, M. 16
Shkrebneva, Lyudmila 89
Short, Philip 53–54
Sigismund von Herberstein, Baron 77
Silver, Nate 9–10
Snyder, Timothy 25–26
socialist countries, safety net in 63–64
social media 22, 52, 127
social safety net 63–64
Society for Psychoanalysis and Psychoanalytic Psychology 109
Sophie (German princess) 78
South Africa 20
South African Commission on Truth and Reconciliation 20, 133
Soviet Union: breakup of 45–46, 79; as communist country 30; disintegration of as narcissistic injury 63, 64; effects of fragmentation of 62–64;

Manchuria, invasion of 16; "nations" (ethnic-centered states) 79; "nostalgia" for 63; post-war contact with West in 1960s 78–79; social safety net 63–64. *See also* Russia
splitting 2, 10, 19, 30–32
Stalin, Josef 37, 41, 42–44, 51, 81, 103; counterattack on German forces 78; and Orthodox Church 66; Putin's imitation of 93
Stalingrad (Grossman) 78
Stalingrad, Battle of 43–44
Stalinism 42–44
Stone, Oliver 47–51
"strong leader," 63–64
suicide 94–95
"Super-ethnos," 97
Sweden 40, 54; and Peter the Great 77–78
symbol analysis 84

Taliban 54, 62
Tatars and Mongols 95
Thatcher, Margaret 46, 52
therapeutic relationship 30–31
This is Not Propaganda: Adventures in the War Against Reality (Pomerantsev) 51–52
time collapse 90–91, 95
Tito, Josip Broz 64
Tolstoy, Leo 123
totalitarian trauma and totalitarian inertia 90
trauma: "chosen," 94–95; intergenerational 1–2, 32–33, 35–37, 53, 75–76, 130; in Putin's' childhood 29; of replacement children 33, 88; unconscious communication of 35–36; undigested 95
traumatic reenactment 36, 130
Truman, Harry 14–16
Trump, Donald 2, 9–13; concern with getting attention 11; hate crimes associated with county votes 104–105; Hitler admired by 104; Mental Functioning ratings 103, 112–118, **113**; no confidence expressed in 112; personality of supporters 104; as treasonous 105
trust 8, 13–14, 24; epistemic trust (ET) 21–22. *See also* truth
truth 7–28, 127, 128, 133; epistemic trust (ET) 21–22; forgiveness and forgetting, role in 19–20; "good" and "bad" people 7, 10; historical evidence overwhelmed by myths 16; importance of 21; loss of interest in 47; new considerations for knowledge acquisition 22–23; "post-truth," 22; quest for 1; Rwandan reconciliation 20–21, 26; told by most people 20; and trust 8, 13–14. *See also* lies; trust
Tskhinvali (South Ossetia) 92
Turkey 89
Turkish Empire 66–67
Tutu, Desmond 20, 26, 133
"Tutzing formula," 46
Tver City 86–87

Ukraine *39*; Azov Battalion 70; and Catherine II 78; *Decree No. 117/2021* 65; earlier wars 38; Holodomor 92, iii; invasions of 92; Kyiv in Russian history 63, 66, 80; natural resources of 61, 68–69; neo-Nazi groups in 69–70; refugees in 38; and religious schism 40–41, 65–68
Ukraine, Putin's invasion of 12, 29, 105; American intelligence services warnings 79–80; approval ratings for Putin 67–68; as battle for the ages 75; de-Nazification linked to 40, 43, 69–70, 93; and leader-follower relationships 83–100; narratives, dismissal of 69–71; and NATO 3, 41–42; NATO as conflict trigger 64–65; provoked by Western breach of commitments 3; Putin's motivations for 79–82; Putin's wish to "reunify" Ukraine with Russia 36, 39; short war anticipated 81; speeches given by Putin 43–44; support for 80–81; West as motivation for 42–43, 127–128; Western blockades, consideration of 80; Western role in responsibility for 44–45, 54
Ukrainian General Staff (UGS) 105
umuganda (reconciliation process, Rwanda) 20
unconscious: "agitated" internal world 43, 84; in Dostoyevsky 124–125; processes 30; repressed or "forgotten" memories 2–3, 35–36. *See also* defense mechanisms; repetition compulsions
unconscious fantasies 32–33, 85, 88–89. *See also* rescue fantasies

United Nations 9; International Criminal Tribunal for the former Yugoslavia 97
United Nations Security Council 47
United States: Constitution 23; Hiroshima and Nagasaki bombing 14–16; illegal, unethical, and amoral events initiated by 8, 13–14; images of conveyed to American people 14; imperialism 8; Insurrection of January 6, 2021 21, 25, 105; intelligence services 79–80; and Nord Stream Pipeline 46–47; presidential lies 8–14; Putin's hand forced by 42–43; Putin's sense of not being heard by 50–51; Russian people overlooked by 51–52; senators, trait ratings for 106; trust in 8–9
United States-Soviet Union dynamics 15–16
unwanted realities, ignoring of 75, 79–80
USS Kitty Hawk 15
USS Maddox 16–17
USS Turner Joy 16

Vietnam: *Maddox* incident 16–17; My Lai Massacre 18–19, 25, 47
Virtues, Democracy, and Online Media: Epistemic Issues (Snow and Vaccarezza) 22
Visser, A. 116
Vladimir the Great of Kyiv 76, 81
Volk, A. 116

Wagner, Mark 21
Wall Street Journal 45

war crimes 51, 81, 97, 105
Warsaw Pact nations 54
Washington Post Fact Checker 11
"We Remember Them All by Name" organization 86
West: as motivation for invasion of Ukraine 42–43; and responsibility for Ukraine war 44–45, 54. *See also* North Atlantic Treaty Organization, (NATO)
Westerners: difficulty in understanding Putin's experiences 29–30
Winter Olympics (2014, Sochi) 123
World War I 15, 61
World War II: education of children about 90–91; as Great Patriotic War 76, 90; "Great Victory" 70th anniversary 91: Hiroshima and Nagasaki bombing 14–16. *See also* Leningrad, Siege of

Xu, X. 104

Yanukovych, Viktor 93
Yeltsin, Boris 89, 95
Yugoslavia, Socialist Federal Republic of 63–64, 67

Zarubina, Zoya 94
Zelensky, Volodymyr 12, 37, 65, 79–80; Mental Functioning ratings 103, 112–118, **113**

For Product Safety Concerns and Information please contact our EU representative GPSR@taylorandfrancis.com
Taylor & Francis Verlag GmbH, Kaufingerstraße 24, 80331 München, Germany

www.ingramcontent.com/pod-product-compliance
Lightning Source LLC
Chambersburg PA
CBHW052134010526
44113CB00036B/2174